The Educator's Epigrams: Learning Lore in Verse for the Enlightened Mind

Riddle Me This: A Professional Exploration in Poetry, Volume 3

Said Al Azri

Published by Said Al Azri, 2024.

While every precaution has been taken in the preparation of this book, the publisher assumes no responsibility for errors or omissions, or for damages resulting from the use of the information contained herein.

THE EDUCATOR'S EPIGRAMS: LEARNING LORE IN VERSE FOR THE ENLIGHTENED MIND

First edition. February 16, 2024.

ISBN: 979-8224755936

Written by Said Al Azri.

Also by Said Al Azri

Classics Reimagined: A Comedic Twist
Echoes of Venice: A Modern Tale of Redemption
Moby-Dick Reversed: A Whale's Humorous Account
Treasure Island: The Parrot's Perspective
Tom Sawyer: The Great Exaggerator
Blunderland Reimagined: Alice's Unique Perspective

Family and Parenting Dynamics
From My Heart to Yours: Messages of Love and Learning for My
Child
Balancing Family Life: Strategies for Modern Parenting

Heartstrings: Tales of Valentine's Verse
Verses of the Heart: A Poetic Journey Through Love's Whimsy
Verses of the Heart 2: A Poetic Journey Through Love's Whimsy

Life, Hobbies, and Careers Series
From Amateur to Applause: A Beginner's Guide to Stand-Up Comedy

This book is lovingly dedicated to

my wife, Maida,

whose unwavering support and insight have been my guiding stars,

and to our children,

who inspire me every day to learn, teach, and appreciate the boundless wonders of education.

May this collection of verses serve as a testament to our shared journey through the landscape of learning.

With endless love, Said

Introduction

Welcome to the enchanting universe of "The Educator's Epigrams: Learning Lore in Verse for the Enlightened Mind," where the noble pursuit of education meets the lyrical grace of poetry in an extraordinary symphony of verse and insight. This book transcends the conventional boundaries of pedagogy, offering a lyrical odyssey through the heart of teaching, learning, and intellectual curiosity.

In an era where education shapes the core of our identities and aspirations, it has blossomed into a wellspring of inspiration for creativity and poetic expression. "The Educator's Epigrams" stands as a beacon of this confluence, presenting a distinctive expedition into the essence of educational philosophy, practices, and the transformative power of learning, all through the elegance and simplicity of poetry.

Within the pages of "The Educator's Epigrams: Learning Lore in Verse for the Enlightened Mind," you will discover a collection of 210 riddle poems, each meticulously woven around a theme or concept from the rich tapestry of education. This compendium is not merely a repository of poetic allure but also a conduit for reflection, dialogue, and the expansion of one's educational and philosophical perspectives. Each riddle poem encapsulates a challenge, an invitation to delve deep into the ethos of education and emerge with a renewed understanding and appreciation for this venerable field.

Whether you are an educator shaping the minds of future generations, a student navigating the waters of knowledge, or simply a lover of words with a thirst for lifelong learning, these poems are designed to kindle your imagination and deepen your reverence for the world of education.

This book is an odyssey for the collective as well as the individual explorer of educational realms, offering an engaging, thoughtful, and enriching experience. From the novice learner to the seasoned pedagogue, each poem serves as a beacon, illuminating the myriad facets of education, encouraging shared discovery, and fostering a community of curious and passionate minds.

As you journey through each verse, familiar concepts from the world of education are reborn as poetic enigmas. From the foundational principles of "Critical Thinking" to the innovative approaches of "Project-Based Learning," from the nurturing care of "Special Needs Education" to the global perspective of "Multicultural Education," each poem is a voyage of discovery, inviting you to embark.

"The Educator's Epigrams" also acts as a bridge, linking those immersed in the academic sphere with those on the periphery. For education professionals, it's an opportunity to gaze upon the familiar landscape through a new, artistic lens. For poetry aficionados and those with a zest for learning, it's a portal to the lyrical beauty residing within educational discourse and practice.

"The Educator's Epigrams" is more than a book; it is a celebration of the fusion between the pedagogic and the poetic, the lesson and the lyric. It is an invitation to pause, reflect, and marvel at the harmony that exists between the world of education and the realm of poetry.

Embark on this unique journey, where each riddle opens doors to both insight and wonder. Decode the ethos of education through the rhythm of poetry and find yourself inspired, challenged, and enlightened.

Welcome, enlightened minds, to a world where wisdom weds wonder.

The Art of Crafting the Riddles:

1. Each riddle thoughtfully captures the essence of educational concepts, designed to engage, entertain, and enlighten readers by blending humor, intrigue, and challenge, making the exploration of educational landscapes both insightful and enjoyable.

2. The riddles serve as playful challenges that encapsulate the significance and roles of educational terms, providing a unique lens through which the evolving field of education can be appreciated and understood more deeply.

3. Aimed at both those familiar with and new to the field of education, these riddle poems encourage a reflective and engaging perspective, highlighting the unique aspects and critical importance of each concept in shaping the educational experience and society.

The Educator's Epigrams

In the realm where wisdom and whimsy entwine,

Lies a book where verse and education align.

"The Educator's Epigrams," a title so grand,

A lyrical journey through learning's vast land.

With riddles and rhymes that dance and delight,

Each page a beacon, each poem a light.

In the world of academia, we often forget,

That joy and discovery can be a sure bet.

Here, educators and learners in verse take a bow,

And subjects once stern, wear a smile now.

From critical thinking to the joy of a class,

Each poem a lesson, in elegance and sass.

In this tome, the binary meets the bard,

Proving that learning is never too hard.

With a stanza for logic, and a verse for the heart,

In education's story, we all play a part.

"Riddle Me This," the series declares,

A professional world, seen through poetic wares.

From IT to medicine, and now to the lore,

Of education's landscape, an open door.

So, welcome all, to this lyrical feast,

Where learning and laughter are never the least.

Through the pages of "The Educator's Epigrams" we'll dive,

Where the enlightened mind comes humorously alive.

Riddle 1

In a realm where knowledge grows,

Where wisdom's seed, each day, is sown,

I stand and guide, but never own,

The minds that wonder, then, they know.

My tools are not of brick or stone,

But patience, love, and gentle tone,

A guide by heart, in minds I roam,

In this great hall, I make them shown.

Who am I, with care so deep,

Awakening minds from their sleep?

Not just a job, a call so steep,

In hearts and souls, what do I keep?

Riddle 2

Where halls echo with tales of old,

And walls are lined with futures bold,

A place where young and eager meet,

To learn of victories and defeat.

With bells that ring to start the day,

In rooms where bright young minds will stray,

To worlds beyond, they take the leap,

With knowledge vast, they sow and reap.

What am I, with doors wide open,

A place where the word is spoken?

A treasure chest for those who seek,

A peak where minds reach their peak.

Riddle 3

In the heart of the year, when the sun stands high,

And the classrooms and hallways all say goodbye.

A time for rest, a time for play,

When books are closed, and out we stray.

Fields and beaches, far and wide,

Becoming the stage for memories to reside.

No bells to ring, no tests to take,

In this golden time, adventures awake.

A pause in learning, or so it seems,

For life teaches much, in these sunlit dreams.

What am I, a seasonal peak,

A hiatus where the spirited seek?

Riddle 4

Eager eyes and open minds,

In me, a world of knowledge finds.

A seeker of truths, old and new,

On a quest to understand and construe.

From letters to numbers, I chase,

Through history and space, I race.

A vessel of potential, yet to be filled,

With dreams and skills, I'm willed.

In halls of learning, my journey begins,

Facing challenges, I aim for wins.

What am I, young and bright,

Igniting the future with every light?

Riddle 5

Bound in cover, spine so tight,

Within me lies a world so bright.

Pages filled with tales untold,

Of heroes brave and villains bold.

I travel lands, both near and far,

From Earth to the edge of the farthest star.

A treasure trove of wisdom, I keep,

In my realm, no knowledge is too deep.

In hands I'm held, in minds I bloom,

Transporting readers beyond their room.

What am I, a portal wide,

Where words and dreams together glide?

Riddle 6

On shoulders young, I rest and ride,

Filled with tools for the learning tide.

Books and pencils, within me dwell,

Secrets and stories, too many to tell.

Each day, I journey, door to door,

A companion in the quest for more.

A carrier of burdens, light and heavy,

Keeping treasures safe and ready.

What am I, sturdy and snug,

A scholar's friend, without a shrug?

Riddle 7

With a rumble and a roar, I awake,

Carrying dreams, no path I forsake.

Down the streets and roads, I travel,

Through seasons that unravel.

A vessel of chatter, of laughter and cheer,

A guardian of youth, year after year.

My seats, a canvas of stories untold,

Of mornings early and evenings cold.

What am I, yellow and bright,

A beacon of learning, in morning light?

Riddle 8

In front of the room, I stand proud and tall,

A witness to questions, big and small.

On my surface, the chalk dances,

Capturing lessons, chances, glances.

A canvas of knowledge, from A to Z,

Where equations and words, freely, spree.

Erasable, yet memorable,

In classrooms, I'm indispensable.

What am I, black or green, wide and tall,

A stage for learning, for one and for all?

Riddle 9

By the light of the moon, I come alive,

Tasks and questions strive to thrive.

In the quiet of the night, I'm tackled,

With books and pens, I'm wrestled.

A bridge between school and home,

Continuing the quest to know and roam.

A challenge, a task, a duty so prime,

Teaching discipline, time after time.

What am I, given daily, a learner's feat,

A nightly journey, until complete?

Riddle 10

Pages upon pages, lined with facts,

A foundation of knowledge, no fiction lacks.

Through chapters and sections, a journey I weave,

From the universe's edge to the atoms we perceive.

A guide, a tutor, silent yet profound,

In classrooms and libraries, I am found.

A constant companion through academic years,

Witness to growth, efforts, and tears.

What am I, a pillar of the class,

A cornerstone of learning, no student shall pass?

Riddle 11

A realm where young minds converge and meet,

A space where knowledge and life greet.

With walls that echo with ideas and questions,

Here, we forge lifelong impressions.

A stage for discovery, play, and talk,

Where thoughts are encouraged to walk.

Chairs and desks, neatly arrayed,

For every lesson, the foundation is laid.

What am I, with doors always ajar,

A cradle of future stars, near and far?

Riddle 12

The captain of the ship, guiding through the sea,

Of education's vast, boundless spree.

A leader, a guide, with vision so keen,

Ensuring the journey's smooth and serene.

With wisdom and patience, decisions are made,

In their presence, doubts fade.

A pillar of strength, for all to see,

Setting the course, for what will be.

What am I, with a role so critical,

At the helm of learning, I stand, pivotal?

Riddle 13

A map of learning, detailed and clear,

Guiding the journey, far and near.

With objectives and goals, so finely spun,

Ensuring that by the end, understanding is won.

A blueprint for discovery, exploration, and fun,

Marking the path, until the lesson is done.

A tool for the teacher, so essential,

Crafting experiences, truly potential.

What am I, crafted with care,

A teacher's guide, beyond compare?

Riddle 14

A woven tapestry of knowledge and skill,

Spanning subjects, vast and still.

A guide for learning, year to year,

Ensuring that all essential knowledge is near.

A framework, robust, guiding the way,

Through the intricacies of each day.

Foundational, expansive, a guiding light,

In the pursuit of wisdom, might.

What am I, so comprehensive and grand,

The educational journey, across the land?

Riddle 15

A test of knowledge, a measure of skill,

In silence, the room, it does fill.

Questions await, to challenge the mind,

Answers to seek, solutions to find.

A culmination of learning, a moment so true,

Revealing what is known, and what to review.

A hurdle, a challenge, to pass and to prove,

In the quest for knowledge, to improve.

What am I, a trial of one's lore,

A gauge of learning, at the core?

Riddle 16

A snapshot of understanding, quick and keen,

A mini-test, not always foreseen.

With questions few, it comes to test,

What's been learned, and what's been guessed.

A check-in, a pulse, on progress made,

On the journey of learning, a small parade.

Lighter than exams, yet important still,

In the fabric of education, it fits the bill.

What am I, brief yet insightful,

A gauge of learning, not to be frightful?

Riddle 17

An act of engaging, with mind so keen,

In books and notes, knowledge is gleaned.

A pursuit of understanding, deep and vast,

Preparing for the future, and learning from the past.

A dedication of time, a focus so true,

To master the old and discover the new.

In silence and thought, insights awake,

The power of learning, at stake.

What am I, an endeavor so pure,

In the quest for knowledge, the cure?

Riddle 18

A flow of knowledge, from one to many,

Information shared, profound and plenty.

A voice that guides, through complex themes,

Illuminating subjects, like light beams.

In halls and rooms, listeners gather,

To learn of worlds, and matters rather.

A traditional method, tried and true,

In the landscape of education, a familiar view.

What am I, a delivery of thought,

Where wisdom and insight are sought?

Riddle 19

A symbol, a letter, marking the score,

Reflecting the effort, knowledge, and more.

A measure of achievement, high or low,

Guiding the learner, on where to go.

In reports and records, it does appear,

A summary of performance, year to year.

A motivator, a guide, in the quest to excel,

In the narrative of learning, it does tell.

What am I, a mark of one's feat,

In the journey of education, a seat?

Riddle 20

A document of progress, detailed and clear,

Marking the journey, far and near.

With grades and comments, it does tell,

The story of learning, where we excel.

A summary of achievements, and areas to grow,

Guiding the next steps, in the learning flow.

Received with anticipation, and sometimes fear,

A reflection of efforts, throughout the year.

What am I, a bearer of news,

In the cycle of education, a muse?

Riddle 21

A journey of the mind, boundless and free,

A quest for wisdom, for you and me.

Through lessons and trials, we seek to find,

The treasures of knowledge, left behind.

Not just in books, but in every encounter,

In every challenge, every ponder.

A lifetime's pursuit, never to cease,

In its quest, we find our peace.

What am I, a path so wide,

Where minds awaken, and truths abide?

Riddle 22

A gift of chance, for those who seek,

To learn, to grow, to climb the peak.

Not just a fund, but a door ajar,

To dreams and goals, near and far.

Awarded to those, with merit and need,

Helping them forward, their dreams to feed.

A beacon of hope, in the academic sea,

Offering passage, making learning free.

What am I, a key so bright,

Unlocking futures, with its light?

Riddle 23

A haven of silence, walls lined with tales,

A world within worlds, where adventure prevails.

From floor to ceiling, knowledge does stack,

In this quiet sanctuary, nothing does lack.

A custodian of history, a keeper of lore,

With each book opened, you'll discover more.

A refuge for seekers, a treasure chest to explore,

In its sacred halls, wisdom pours.

What am I, a home for the book,

A place for those, who come to look?

Riddle 24

A companion in learning, slender and fine,

Holding thoughts, ideas, line by line.

On its pages, ink flows free,

Capturing whispers of what might be.

A canvas blank, for minds to paint,

Memories and knowledge, without restraint.

Through lectures and studies, it faithfully stays,

A keeper of insights, through the days.

What am I, bound and neat,

A collection of pages, thoughts complete?

Riddle 25

A tool so simple, yet mighty in hand,

Crafting worlds, at your command.

With graphite heart, encased in wood,

It writes the future, as it should.

In strokes and shades, it brings to life,

Ideas and dreams, cutting like a knife.

Erasable marks, it does concede,

Allowing for change, as you proceed.

What am I, slender and gray,

A writer of tales, in leaden array?

Riddle 26

A station for thought, for work, for play,

A constant through the academic fray.

Sturdy and steadfast, it holds the weight,

Of books and papers, early and late.

A personal space, for young minds to grow,

A stage for learning, in the academic show.

In classrooms aligned, in rows so neat,

A foundation for learning, a student's seat.

What am I, four-legged and firm,

A scholar's altar, long-term?

Riddle 27

A task designed, to challenge the mind,

In its completion, knowledge you'll find.

A piece of the puzzle, in learning's grand plan,

Testing your grasp, since it began.

From essays to problems, projects wide,

It's a measure of learning, you cannot hide.

A step in the journey, to understand,

The concepts and skills, at hand.

What am I, a duty, a quest,

In pursuit of education, a test?

Riddle 28

A structured journey, through a field of study,

Where minds engage, thoughts become muddy.

A series of lessons, designed to impart,

Knowledge and skills, from the start.

A path through academia, clearly defined,

In its completion, enlightenment you'll find.

A segment of learning, a part of the whole,

Nurturing wisdom, fulfilling a role.

What am I, a passage of learning, set and clear,

A voyage of knowledge, year by year?

Riddle 29

A parchment of achievement, earned and bestowed,

Marking the end of a journey, a road.

A symbol of mastery, in a field so chosen,

Of challenges faced, and obstacles frozen.

Not just a paper, but a key to the door,

Of opportunities, careers, and so much more.

A testament to dedication, and toil,

A reward for the years of turmoil.

What am I, a credential, a prize,

A culmination of efforts, under the skies?

Riddle 30

A celebration of completion, a rite so grand,

For all the learners, across the land.

A milestone reached, a chapter ends,

As into the world, each one wends.

Cap and gown, and tassels sway,

Marking the passage, to a new day.

A gathering of cheers, of tears, of joy,

For every graduate, girl and boy.

What am I, an occasion so bright,

A turning of pages, into the light?

Riddle 31

A guide, not in the front, but by your side,

In struggles and questions, I'm your guide.

With patience and wisdom, I pave the way,

For understanding, in a personalized array.

Not bound by classrooms, nor by bell,

In learning's journey, I help you dwell.

A mentor, a coach, for your academic quest,

Ensuring that you give your very best.

What am I, with knowledge to impart,

A helper in learning, an educational art?

Riddle 32

A roadmap of courses, detailed and clear,

Outlining the journey, far and near.

From topics to readings, assignments, and tests,

It sets the expectations, no surprises, no jests.

A contract of sorts, between teacher and class,

Guiding the semester, as weeks pass.

A preview of knowledge, soon to be explored,

A promise of learning, intellectually adored.

What am I, a guide at the start,

A framework of learning, part by part?

Riddle 33

A cycle of learning, divided in phases,

Through autumn and winter, and spring it blazes.

A rhythm of studies, a structured span,

Where courses and lessons, in sequence, plan.

From the first bell in fall, to summer's release,

A period of growth, knowledge's increase.

A timeline for students, and teachers alike,

Marking the passage, of academic hike.

What am I, a yearly round,

In schools and colleges, I'm found?

Riddle 34

A division of time, half a year in length,

A structure for learning, offering strength.

With a start and an end, a break in between,

A pace for education, well-routined.

A term where courses are tightly packed,

Where exams and projects are interacted.

A segment of the academic year,

Where knowledge is gained, and challenges are near.

What am I, a portion so defined,

In education's cycle, intertwined?

Riddle 35

A pause in the march, of academic strive,

A time to relax, to rejuvenate, to revive.

In the season of growth, a well-deserved rest,

From studies and exams, a temporary nest.

A week or two, where no lectures are heard,

A break from the routine, universally preferred.

A moment in spring, to catch one's breath,

Before the final push, to academic wealth.

What am I, a hiatus so brief,

In the academic calendar, a relief?

Riddle 36

A place of higher learning, beyond the basic need,

Where specialized knowledge, one can heed.

With programs diverse, and degrees to pursue,

A step towards dreams, making them true.

A community smaller, where close bonds are formed,

In classrooms and campuses, minds are transformed.

A preparation for careers, a stage of life's quest,

Where skills are honed, and characters are test.

What am I, a gateway so wide,

To futures bright, with knowledge as guide?

Riddle 37

A bastion of knowledge, research, and learning,

Where curiosity's fire, keeps on burning.

With faculties broad, and degrees of all kinds,

A universe of disciplines, it binds.

A center for scholars, students, and thought,

Where future leaders, are shaped and wrought.

More than just education, a community so vast,

A place where the foundations, of careers are cast.

What am I, grand and diverse,

A pinnacle of learning, the universe?

Riddle 38

A fusion of learning, with digital grace,

Transforming the classroom, into a new space.

With tools and platforms, learning's expanded,

Boundaries of knowledge, constantly banded.

From apps to software, virtual realms to explore,

Making education accessible, more and more.

A revolution in teaching, and how we learn,

Innovation's fire, continues to burn.

What am I, a blend so unique,

Tech's power in education, we seek?

Riddle 39

A classroom without walls, in the digital age,

Where knowledge meets tech, on the virtual stage.

Accessible to all, far and wide,

A revolution in education, with a global stride.

From videos to forums, lessons come alive,

Allowing learning, anytime, to thrive.

A flexible path, for those who seek,

Knowledge and skills, unique and sleek.

What am I, without a physical bound,

In the internet's expanse, I'm found?

Riddle 40

Not confined by geography, a bridge so long,

Connecting learners to knowledge, making them strong.

Through mail, video, or the web, lessons are sent,

Breaking barriers, making education omnipresent.

A mode of learning, flexible and wide,

For those who work, or must stay aside.

Providing access to education, far and near,

Opening doors, overcoming the barrier of fear.

What am I, a reach so far,

Bringing closer, the educational star?

Riddle 41

In the quiet of pages, a journey begins,

Where stories and knowledge are twins.

Through symbols and letters, the mind takes flight,

Discovering worlds, hidden from sight.

A skill so vital, from early age,

Unlocking the wisdom of every page.

A gateway to places, both far and near,

In the realm of words, I steer.

What am I, an activity so profound,

In books and texts, I'm found?

Riddle 42

With pen in hand, I come to life,

Crafting worlds, in joy and strife.

A form of expression, so unique and bold,

Telling tales, new and old.

A skill so essential, in education's core,

From letters to essays, and so much more.

An art and a discipline, combined as one,

Where thoughts and ideas, are spun.

What am I, a creation so bright,

Bringing thoughts to form, in black and white?

Riddle 43

The foundation of numbers, so clear and true,

Where addition and subtraction, are just the preview.

Multiplication, division, the building blocks,

In this domain, logic talks.

A branch of mathematics, so pure and raw,

In its simplicity, wonder and awe.

A skill so crucial, in every land,

Where numbers and figures, go hand in hand.

What am I, a discipline so basic,

In the world of math, I'm classic?

Riddle 44

A quest for truth, in the natural world,

Where mysteries and wonders are unfurled.

From atoms to galaxies, life to light,

Exploring the universe, with keen insight.

A subject so vast, it branches wide,

Physics, chemistry, biology, side by side.

A foundation of knowledge, empirical and keen,

Where evidence and experiment, are seen.

What am I, a field so broad,

In the pursuit of knowledge, toward?

Riddle 45

A tapestry of time, woven with events,

Where past and present, make sense.

A story of humanity, in triumph and defeat,

In its lessons, wisdom we meet.

A subject that teaches, of times gone by,

Of cultures and empires, under the sky.

An exploration of origins, and how we came to be,

In the pages of time, a vast sea.

What am I, a narrative so grand,

In the chronicles of time, I stand?

Riddle 46

A study of Earth, its lands, and seas,

Of climates, countries, and the trees.

A subject that explores, the physical and more,

Human interactions, at its core.

From mountains to rivers, cities to plains,

Understanding the world, and its many domains.

A field that connects us, to the world at large,

In the quest for knowledge, I charge.

What am I, a discipline so wide,

In the exploration of Earth, I guide?

Riddle 47

A realm of expression, so vast and free,

Where creativity meets, in harmony.

From painting to sculpture, photography too,

In this field, imagination brews.

A subject that teaches, the beauty of sight,

In colors and forms, a delight.

An exploration of human emotion and thought,

In the canvas of culture, battles fought.

What am I, a creation so bold,

In the spectrum of beauty, I hold?

Riddle 48

A language universal, in rhythm and rhyme,

Transcending boundaries, of place and time.

From melody to harmony, in notes it speaks,

In the soul of humanity, it seeks.

An art that touches, the heart and mind,

In its composition, emotions bind.

A subject that teaches, the power of song,

In the chorus of life, we belong.

What am I, an expression so deep,

In the harmony of the world, I sweep?

Riddle 49

A field of learning, where movement is key,

Promoting health, vitality, and glee.

From sports to fitness, activities abound,

In this subject, energy is found.

Teaching the value, of staying active and fit,

In the journey of life, a perfect hit.

A curriculum of strength, endurance, and fun,

Under the roof of the gym, or under the sun.

What am I, a lesson in action,

In the wellness of life, a fraction?

Riddle 50

An adventure outside, the classroom's bound,

Where learning and experience, are found.

To museums, parks, or historic sites,

In these journeys, education ignites.

A hands-on approach, to see and touch,

Making subjects alive, matters as such.

An escape from books, into the real,

Where the textures of knowledge, one can feel.

What am I, an excursion so grand,

In the world of learning, a firsthand?

Riddle 51

A realm where logic and numbers reign,

A universe with its own domain.

From simple equations to complex theories,

A language of patterns, in its queries.

A discipline both ancient and vast,

Where the quest for truth holds fast.

In its embrace, the world makes sense,

A testament to intellect's immense.

What am I, a study so pure,

Where through numbers, solutions endure?

Riddle 52

The study of life, in all its forms,

From single cells to complex storms.

A look at existence, through a microscope,

In its wonder, forever we hope.

From genetics to ecosystems wide,

In this science, life's secrets hide.

A field where the living, unite and divide,

In the dance of nature, we take pride.

What am I, a science so grand,

Where life's mysteries, we understand?

Riddle 53

A world of atoms, molecules in bond,

A quest for reactions, of which we're fond.

From elements on the table, a periodic array,

To compounds and changes, in display.

The study of matter, and its transformations,

In labs and beakers, our fascinations.

A bridge between the physical and life,

In its essence, both harmony and strife.

What am I, a science so keen,

Where the building blocks of life are seen?

Riddle 54

The laws of nature, here we explore,

From gravity's pull to quantum lore.

A universe governed by forces and motion,

In its study, we find devotion.

From the smallest particle, to the vast cosmic,

In this realm, the truth's atomic.

A foundation of science, broad and deep,

In its principles, the secrets we keep.

What am I, a study profound,

Where the universe's rules are found?

Riddle 55

A world of words, where stories unfold,

Of human experience, new and old.

In poetry and prose, emotions dance,

In the power of narrative, we take our chance.

A study of texts, rich and diverse,

Through them, the human soul we converse.

An exploration of culture, and human thought,

In its tapestry, wisdom is caught.

What am I, an art so dear,

Where through words, the human heart we hear?

Riddle 56

The mastery of words, in reading and write,

Where communication shines so bright.

From grammar to rhetoric, in eloquence we trust,

In the power of language, it's a must.

A discipline that shapes, how we express,

Our ideas, our dreams, and how we address.

A foundation of education, clear and strong,

In its practice, we find our voice, our song.

What am I, a field so vast,

Where in the power of language, our anchor's cast?

Riddle 57

A look at societies, and how they're woven,

In history, geography, economics, notions proven.

A study of people, and their relations,

In its lessons, the foundation of nations.

A field that explores, the human condition,

In its diversity, and shared mission.

From past to present, a journey we take,

In the quest for understanding, for humanity's sake.

What am I, a study so wide,

Where in the fabric of society, we reside?

Riddle 58

A study of Earth, and its systems so vast,

Where concerns for the future, link to the past.

From climate change to conservation's quest,

In its embrace, our survival's test.

An interdisciplinary field, so keen,

Where the health of our planet, is seen.

A call to action, and understanding,

In its knowledge, our future's demanding.

What am I, a science so true,

Where for the Earth, a guardian's view?

Riddle 59

A realm of algorithms, and coding's might,

Where in binary, we find delight.

From software to hardware, a digital domain,

In its logic, solutions we ascertain.

A study of computing, so vast and deep,

In its language, the future we seek.

A field that shapes, the modern age,

In its script, the world's stage.

What am I, a discipline so key,

Where through technology, possibilities we see?

Riddle 60

The backbone of the digital world, so vast,

Where networks and systems, our messages are cast.

From data management to cybersecurity's fight,

In its realm, keeping the digital world bright.

A field that ensures, the flow of info remains,

In its hands, the digital pulse sustains.

A study of technologies, that connect and protect,

In its skill, the modern world we reflect.

What am I, an essential craft,

In the age of information, a raft?

Riddle 61

In the halls of learning, a guide stands true,

A confidant for problems, old and new.

With an open door and a listening ear,

For every student, they're always near.

A navigator through academic seas,

And personal storms, with equal ease.

In choices and challenges, they lend a hand,

Ensuring no one alone must stand.

What am I, a support so vital,

In the journey of education, a title?

Riddle 62

Beyond the books and classroom tests,

Lies a world of pursuits, where passion nests.

From arts to science, sports to speech,

In these endeavors, new heights we reach.

A balance to studies, in learning's quest,

Here, talents and interests manifest.

A part of schooling, not in the core,

But in these moments, character is more.

What am I, a pursuit so grand,

In the spectrum of growth, I stand?

Riddle 63

A group of thinkers, sharp and keen,

Where arguments are built, and fallacies seen.

In the arena of words, they contend and spar,

Honing skills that will carry them far.

A crucible of logic, reason, and poise,

Where every word counts, and precision joys.

A team where the art of persuasion is key,

In the battle of minds, they're free.

What am I, a collective so bright,

In the dialectics of debate, our might?

Riddle 64

On fields and courts, together we stand,

In pursuit of victory, hand in hand.

A brotherhood and sisterhood, in sport and sweat,

Lessons in teamwork, we'll never forget.

Through wins and losses, our spirits soar,

In the game of life, it's so much more.

A school's pride, in jerseys and cheers,

In every match, overcoming fears.

What am I, a unit so tight,

In the spirit of competition, our flight?

Riddle 65

A gathering of minds, with interests alike,

In subjects and hobbies, passion strikes.

From robotics to art, in diversity we thrive,

In these meetings, our curiosities come alive.

A mini-community within school's gates,

Where inquiry and friendship await.

A place for exploration, beyond the class,

In the joy of learning, we surpass.

What am I, a group so engaged,

In the pursuit of interests, we're caged?

Riddle 66

A stage of dreams, where stories are told,

In costumes and lines, characters bold.

A collective effort, where talents shine,

In the act of performing, we intertwine.

A break from routine, an artistic escape,

Where students and teachers, a new world shape.

Drama and laughter, in lights and sound,

In this performance, our spirits are found.

What am I, an event so bright,

In the realm of theater, our delight?

Riddle 67

With instruments in hand, we come together,

Creating music, in all types of weather.

From brass to woodwind, percussion to strings,

In our harmony, the heart sings.

A part of school life, in marches and shows,

In the rhythm of unity, our camaraderie grows.

A musical journey, where skills are honed,

In the language of melodies, we're owned.

What am I, a collective in tune,

In the orchestra of education, our boon?

Riddle 68

Voices united, in harmony and song,

Where every note, every chord belongs.

In the blend of pitches, a story we tell,

In the power of singing, we dwell.

From alto to soprano, bass to tenor,

In our chorus, no one is a foreigner.

A musical ensemble, in joy and in plight,

In the choir, our souls take flight.

What am I, a group so vast,

In the symphony of voices, our cast?

Riddle 69

A gathering of all, in the hall so wide,

Where announcements and honors coincide.

A communal moment, in the school's day,

Where we listen, learn, and sometimes play.

A forum for voices, a space to share,

In the unity of school spirit, we care.

A regular pause, from the academic chase,

In this collective space, our community's base.

What am I, a meeting so grand,

In the heart of school life, I stand?

Riddle 70

A bridge between homes and educational halls,

Where together, we answer schooling's calls.

In collaboration, we seek to enhance,

The quality of learning, and every child's chance.

A forum for discussion, a partnership true,

In the welfare of students, our aim is to pursue.

Through fundraisers and meetings, our efforts unite,

In the mission of education, we ignite.

What am I, a union so key,

In the fabric of school community, we be?

Riddle 71

A tailored path, where needs are met,

With care and support, the goals are set.

For those who learn, in their own way,

In our dedication, their potential lay.

Not left behind, but rather, embraced,

In the spectrum of learning, uniquely placed.

A testament to diversity, in education's heart,

Where every student plays a part.

What am I, a program so refined,

In the embrace of all minds, you'll find?

Riddle 72

A philosophy, where all belong,

In the tapestry of school, a vibrant song.

Differences celebrated, strengths recognized,

Where barriers fall, and spirits are prized.

A commitment to equity, in every class,

Ensuring no student is bypassed.

Together we learn, together we grow,

In the garden of education, diversity we sow.

What am I, a principle so dear,

In the unity of learning, we steer?

Riddle 73

A challenge in the way, some minds process,

Not lesser, but different, in the educational quest.

With understanding and strategies, we bridge the gap,

Ensuring every learner, is on the map.

A recognition, that not all paths are the same,

In the journey of knowledge, no blame.

A call for empathy, support, and care,

In the landscape of learning, a fair share.

What am I, a condition to understand,

In the embrace of education, a helping hand?

Riddle 74

A document crafted, with care and thought,

For learners unique, a plan wrought.

Goals and supports, laid out clear,

To ensure success, year by year.

A collaborative effort, team-wide,

Where student progress, is the guide.

Tailored teaching, interventions right,

In the quest for learning, a guiding light.

What am I, a plan so precise,

In special education, a device?

Riddle 75

A program designed, for minds that soar,

Where challenges meet, and spirits roar.

For those who excel, beyond the norm,

In their education, we transform.

Enrichment and acceleration, we provide,

Ensuring their talents, do not hide.

A nurturing of potential, so vast,

In the realm of learning, they're cast.

What am I, an initiative so bright,

For exceptional learners, a flight?

Riddle 76

A measure of knowledge, skills, and more,

Across the board, scores we pore.

A common ground, for assessment's sake,

In education's landscape, a stake.

Objective and uniform, in its aim,

Across students, the conditions the same.

A gauge of learning, a tool of compare,

In the quest for quality, a fair share.

What am I, a test so wide,

In education's journey, a guide?

Riddle 77

A test of readiness, for college's door,

Math, reading, and writing, core.

A benchmark for admission, far and wide,

In students' futures, a guide.

Not just a score, but a step towards dreams,

In the landscape of higher education, it seems.

A rite of passage, for many to take,

In the journey of learning, a stake.

What am I, a test so known,

In college admissions, a tone?

Riddle 78

Another gateway, to education's next stage,

Assessing skills, page by page.

English, math, reading, and science in tow,

For college-bound students, a way to show.

A score that reflects, potential and preparation,

In the quest for college, a declaration.

An alternative path, to college's gate,

In the landscape of futures, a weight.

What am I, a test with a mission,

In higher education, a tradition?

Riddle 79

A program offering, college-level courses deep,

In high school halls, college credits to reap.

Rigorous and challenging, a test at the end,

On success, college credits, they lend.

A bridge between stages, of education's path,

For students ambitious, a rigorous bath.

An opportunity to excel, to stand out,

In the journey of learning, a clout.

What am I, a program so bold,

In advanced learning, a mold?

Riddle 80

A global curriculum, broad and wide,

Where inquiry and understanding, coincide.

For students around the world, a holistic view,

In learning's journey, a path anew.

Critical thinking, a global context,

In education's realm, a complex text.

A diploma respected, across the land,

In the quest for knowledge, a grand stand.

What am I, a program so diverse,

In global education, a universe?

Riddle 81

The price of knowledge, the cost of class,

For lectures, labs, and credits to amass.

A gateway fee, to learning's realm,

With books and resources, at the helm.

A sum that opens the door to dreams,

Where the future's brighter than it seems.

In this investment, hopes are woven,

By this pledge, many paths are chosen.

Not just a number, but an investment grand,

In future's promise, in dreams planned.

What am I, asked by schools wide and far,

For education's journey, a guiding star?

Riddle 82

A beacon of hope, for those in need,

Making education's path, a possibility indeed.

Grants, loans, and work-study, a blend,

On this support, many depend.

Easing the burden, lifting the weight,

For many, I unlock education's gate.

Aiding dreams to take flight and soar,

In pursuit of knowledge, to explore.

A bridge over waters, financially deep,

Ensuring that dreams, one can keep.

What am I, a hand extended, so bright,

In the pursuit of knowledge, a light?

Riddle 83

A reward for merit, for talent so bright,

Easing the burden of tuition's might.

A recognition of achievement, and need,

Helping students to succeed.

A beacon for those who excel,

In academic realms where ambitions dwell.

Lifting spirits, granting opportunities new,

For the diligent, a path to pursue.

Not just a gift, but an honor true,

For academic excellence, a due.

What am I, a prize of learning's quest,

In supporting education, I invest?

Riddle 84

A grant for scholars, in research deep,

For study and exploration, a leap.

Not just funding, but a community of minds,

Where in collaboration, one finds.

An alliance of intellects, sharing a quest,

In pursuit of knowledge, never at rest.

Fueling inquiries that span wide and far,

Under the banner of the evening star.

Advanced study, projects so grand,

In this pursuit, together we stand.

What am I, a partnership in discovery,

Aiding knowledge, a scholarly treasury?

Riddle 85

A foray into the professional sphere,

Where theory meets practice, clear.

A stepping stone, for careers to bloom,

In real-world settings, knowledge to consume.

A melding of learning with hands-on task,

In this experience, questions we ask.

Shaping futures with every hour,

In this role, skills empower.

An opportunity to learn, to grow,

In fields chosen, a future to show.

What am I, a bridge between study and vocation,

A practical education, a foundation?

Riddle 86

A culmination of study, a project so grand,

An original research, at command.

A requirement for masters, a proof of might,

In academic pursuit, a shining light.

A quest for knowledge, a journey deep,

Where questions and curiosities leap.

Upon my completion, insights unfurl,

In the academic world, a precious pearl.

A statement of theory, evidence to bind,

In this document, one's passion you'll find.

What am I, a scholar's endeavor,

In the quest for knowledge, a lever?

Riddle 87

An academic manuscript, detailed and long,

The essence of a doctorate, strong.

A contribution to the field, new and keen,

In these pages, a scholar's dream seen.

A testament to years of toil and thought,

With wisdom and discovery fraught.

A journey through the academic night,

Bringing new insights to light.

Years of research, analysis, and review,

To the world of academia, something new.

What am I, a tome of insight,

In the highest education, a flight?

Riddle 88

A seal of approval, a mark of quality,

Ensuring standards, in the educational facility.

A process rigorous, institutions must pass,

For credibility, and class.

An emblem of trust, for all to see,

A guarantee of what education should be.

Ensuring that learning meets the mark,

Guiding students out of the dark.

A guarantee that education meets the bar,

For students near, and students far.

What am I, a certification so prime,

In the realm of education, a sign?

Riddle 89

Graduates of a place of learning, standing tall,

With memories, experiences, they recall.

A network vast, spanning years and space,

In their alma mater, they find a base.

Once students, now ambassadors proud,

In their achievements, they're avowed.

Carrying forth the legacy of their school,

In life's vast pool, they're a jewel.

Not just former students, but a family wide,

With pride in their journey, they stride.

What am I, a community with a past,

In the fabric of the institution, cast?

Riddle 90

A student in pursuit of a degree first and keen,

In the realm of higher education, seen.

Before the master's or doctorate's call,

This foundational journey, a path for all.

Embarking on a voyage of knowledge and growth,

To question, to learn, to take the oath.

A seeker of truths in a scholarly sea,

In pursuit of what will be, they're free.

A time of learning, of growth so vast,

In these years, foundations are cast.

What am I, a term so known,

In the university's garden, sown?

Riddle 91

In the halls of wisdom, a journey's end,

A title bestowed, honors to extend.

Years of study, nights without rest,

In pursuit of knowledge, a relentless quest.

Caps fly high, in the sky so blue,

A celebration of what you did pursue.

Not just a student, but now more refined,

With a degree in hand, a future defined.

What am I, who has crossed the stage,

With diploma in hand, ready to engage?

A symbol of success, a seeker no more,

In the world of academia, I've scored.

Riddle 92

Beyond the first degree, I seek to climb,

For knowledge deeper, more sublime.

In specialized fields, I delve and dwell,

Pushing boundaries, with stories to tell.

A master's or beyond, a pursuit so keen,

In the realms of academia, I'm seen.

Not just learning, but contributing too,

To the body of knowledge, adding anew.

What am I, with aspirations high,

Seeking truths that in complexity lie?

A scholar, a seeker, in learning's vast sea,

In the quest for more, forever I'll be.

Riddle 93

The pinnacle of academic climb, so steep,

A journey long, where the slopes are deep.

Years of research, a dissertation to defend,

In pursuit of a title, on which careers depend.

A doctor now, in my field so wise,

With expertise, no one denies.

Teaching, researching, leading the way,

In my domain, I have a say.

What am I, with a title so grand,

In academia's ranks, prominently I stand?

A testament to perseverance and intellect's might,

At the summit of learning, I take flight.

Riddle 94

A guardian of knowledge, a mentor so wise,

Under my guidance, students' ambitions rise.

Lectures and seminars, research to lead,

In the quest for understanding, I plant the seed.

Tenured and respected, in my academic home,

Across the world of ideas, freely I roam.

Publishing, presenting, a scholar so bright,

In the quest for knowledge, a guiding light.

What am I, with a title so revered,

In the halls of education, by all endeared?

A pillar of learning, on whom many rely,

In the pursuit of wisdom, my standards are high.

Riddle 95

In classrooms and halls, my voice carries far,

Teaching subjects ranging, from history to a star.

Not just a teacher, but a specialist indeed,

In imparting knowledge, I take the lead.

With passion and expertise, I engage the room,

In the minds of the curious, understanding blooms.

From coursework to exams, my guidance is key,

In the landscape of learning, a crucial spree.

What am I, who lectures with grace,

In the academic world, holding my space?

A conveyor of knowledge, in depth and breadth,

Igniting minds, my teaching's quest.

Riddle 96

In the shadow of academia, a role so vital,

Supporting professors, in tasks so critical.

Grading papers, leading labs, a helping hand,

In the education process, firmly I stand.

A bridge between students and the teaching lead,

In my role, to their success, I heed.

Often a student myself, learning and teaching entwined,

In this dual journey, growth I find.

What am I, in the academic flow,

Supporting the learning process, helping knowledge grow?

A foundational stone in the educational assist,

In the world of teaching, I persist.

Riddle 97

A quest for knowledge, a journey deep,

In labs and libraries, vigils I keep.

Asking questions, seeking answers true,

In the unknown, clues I pursue.

Not just a process, but a passion so bright,

In the pursuit of understanding, my delight.

Publishing findings, in journals and more,

Expanding the horizons of what's in store.

What am I, a pursuit so keen,

Where through inquiry, the unseen is seen?

In the realm of academia, a vital part,

In the expansion of knowledge, I impart.

Riddle 98

A gathering of minds, in discussion deep,

Where ideas and theories, in conversation steep.

Not a lecture, but an exchange so fair,

In the exploration of subjects rare.

With a leader to guide, but not to dictate,

Here, in dialogue, insights we create.

A part of education, where understanding grows,

In these sessions, the essence of inquiry shows.

What am I, a meeting of thought,

In the landscape of learning, a crucial spot?

A space for debate, for learning's sake,

In the journey of knowledge, a path we take.

Riddle 99

A hands-on session, skills to acquire,

In practice and application, we aspire.

Not just theory, but action so bold,

In these gatherings, new abilities unfold.

From writing to coding, arts to science,

In these meetings, on skills, we place reliance.

An integral part of the learning sphere,

In the development of talents, we hold dear.

What am I, practical and wise,

A crucible of learning, under the skies?

In the realm of education, a practical part,

In the craft of skills, a crucial start.

Riddle 100

A symposium of scholars, from near and far,

Presenting research, under academia's star.

In panels and keynotes, knowledge we share,

A community of inquiry, a scholarly affair.

Networking, collaborating, in discussions profound,

In these gatherings, new ideas abound.

An essential part of the academic year,

Where in the exchange of intellect, colleagues cheer.

What am I, a gathering so grand,

In the world of scholarship, a stand?

A beacon of progress, of academic might,

In the pursuit of knowledge, a site.

Riddle 101

In the art and science of teaching, I reside,

A guide on how learning can best be applied.

Not merely instruction, but nurturing the seed,

Of curiosity, understanding, the learner's need.

From theory to practice, strategies so wide,

In my embrace, effective teaching is spied.

Child-centered, active, inquiry-based too,

Adapting to changes, always seeking the new.

What am I, that shapes the way,

We teach the young, day by day?

A term that captures, the heart of education's creed,

In the journey of learning, a guiding lead.

Riddle 102

Focused on adults, in their quest to learn,

Acknowledging the experience they bring in turn.

Self-directed, ready, with goals in sight,

In their lifelong journey, seeking light.

Not just filling vessels, but sparking a flame,

In mature learners, who know the game.

Motivation internal, relevance is key,

In this approach, learning's free.

What am I, the art so profound,

In adult education, where I'm found?

A contrast to pedagogy, yet akin in aim,

Empowering learners, in education's name.

Riddle 103

A blueprint of learning, structured and clear,

Guiding educators, year to year.

Objectives, goals, and assessments align,

Ensuring that instruction, with needs, entwine.

A process ongoing, adapting to change,

Incorporating feedback, within its range.

From knowledge to skills, attitudes too,

Crafting experiences, both old and new.

What am I, a task so grand,

In shaping education, I stand?

A foundation of schools, a strategic plan,

In guiding learning, I lead the van.

Riddle 104

The study of how, humans best learn,

From cognition to development, my concern.

Motivations, challenges, behaviors observed,

In this science, insights are preserved.

Applying theory to practice, in classroom and field,

Helping educators, their methods to wield.

Understanding diversity, in ways we think,

In the fabric of learning, I am the link.

What am I, a field so vast,

In the journey of learning, my cast?

Bridging minds and education, with every test,

Ensuring teaching methods, are the best.

Riddle 105

Visual, auditory, kinesthetic, in blend,

The ways in which, we comprehend.

Not one size fits all, in learning's quest,

But personalized paths, that suit us best.

Acknowledging diversity, in how we perceive,

And in how knowledge, we receive.

A concept that guides, the educational scene,

In teaching strategies, it's keen.

What am I, a theory so broad,

In understanding learning, a guiding rod?

Highlighting differences, in how we learn,

To maximize potential, our concern.

Riddle 106

A mix of traditional, with digital age,

In classrooms and online, I engage.

Maximizing strengths, of each modality,

Offering flexibility, and new reality.

Not confined by walls, or even time,

In this approach, learning's prime.

Enhancing engagement, through diverse means,

In the landscape of education, I gleam.

What am I, a hybrid mode,

In the journey of learning, a broad road?

Combining face-to-face, with online zest,

In the pursuit of teaching, among the best.

Riddle 107

Inverting the norm, where homework and class switch role,

Lectures at home, and in class, control.

Engaging students, in active learning's embrace,

Maximizing classroom time, for an effective pace.

A strategy that encourages, preparation before meet,

Turning passive listening, into something neat.

Discussion, application, in the time we share,

In this model, active engagement is fair.

What am I, a method so keen,

In educational strategies, prominently seen?

Flipping the script, on traditional class,

In the realm of learning, I pass.

Riddle 108

A platform for learning, wide and vast,

Breaking down barriers, of the past.

Accessible to all, without a fee,

In the digital world, education's free.

From philosophy to science, topics abound,

In this format, knowledge is unbound.

Connecting learners, from far and wide,

In the pursuit of education, a global stride.

What am I, a course so grand,

Across the internet, I stand?

Massive in reach, open in scope,

In the landscape of learning, I offer hope.

Riddle 109

Digital classrooms, where knowledge flows,

Beyond the physical, education grows.

Through modules, webinars, interactive tools,

In this domain, learning rules.

A flexible path, for those who seek,

To study anytime, each week.

Advancing skills, or pursuing degrees,

In this format, learners find ease.

What am I, an educational trend,

Where technology and learning blend?

A method of teaching, without a room,

In the digital age, I bloom.

Riddle 110

A room not of bricks, but bytes and light,

Where learners gather, without a physical site.

Interacting, engaging, in real-time or paced,

In this space, education is chased.

Whiteboards, chats, and video streams,

In this environment, learning beams.

A bridge across distances, so vast,

Making education, flexible and vast.

What am I, a classroom so neat,

Where technology and learners meet?

In the realm of the digital, a space so grand,

In the future of education, I stand.

Riddle 111

A digital hub, where courses live,

A place where resources, we give and sieve.

Assignments, grades, and discussions held,

In this system, education's propelled.

Tracking progress, a breeze so fair,

Accessibility, from anywhere.

A cornerstone of e-learning's might,

In this platform, education's light.

What am I, a tool so vast,

In the realm of digital education, I'm cast?

Supporting learning, in ways so grand,

An essential system, at your command.

Riddle 112

Not just present, but actively involved,

In learning's mystery, problems solved.

Participation, interest, curiosity piqued,

In this state, knowledge's peak is reached.

Beyond the surface, deep into the core,

Where learning becomes something more.

A goal for educators, to inspire and ignite,

In this pursuit, education takes flight.

What am I, a concept so key,

In the landscape of learning, a goal to be?

More than attendance, a vibrant interaction,

In the journey of education, a main attraction.

Riddle 113

A check-in on progress, along the way,

Guiding teaching and learning, every day.

Feedback given, to shape the course,

In this approach, learning's force.

Not a final judgment, but a helpful guide,

Showing where understanding may collide.

A tool for improvement, growth's insight,

In this process, education's light.

What am I, an assessment so formative,

In the journey of learning, a supportive narrative?

Helping students grow, before the end,

In the landscape of education, a helpful friend.

Riddle 114

At the journey's end, a final test,

To measure what's learned, at its best.

A culmination of all that's been taught,

In this assessment, achievement's sought.

Not merely a grade, but a summary clear,

Of knowledge gained, throughout the year.

A benchmark of progress, for all to see,

In this method, accountability.

What am I, an evaluation so summative,

In education's cycle, a conclusive narrative?

A final measure, of learning's quest,

In the realm of assessment, among the test.

Riddle 115

A process of critique, from those alike,

Assessing work, with insights strike.

In academia or class, a tool so keen,

Ensuring quality, in what's seen.

Feedback from equals, constructive and fair,

A part of learning, to improve what's there.

A collaborative effort, to refine and enhance,

In this practice, knowledge's advance.

What am I, a method so peer,

In the world of learning, a mirror clear?

A way to improve, through feedback's guide,

In the journey of knowledge, a valuable stride.

Riddle 116

The skill to analyze, question, and reflect,

To discern truth, bias detect.

Not taking at face value, but probing deep,

In this skill, wisdom we reap.

A cornerstone of education, so vital and true,

Encouraging students, perspectives anew.

A foundation for reasoning, and understanding's quest,

In this practice, our minds are best.

What am I, a cognitive skill so prime,

In the landscape of learning, essential every time?

More than memorization, a deeper dive,

In the realm of thought, where we thrive.

Riddle 117

Facing challenges, finding ways through,

Innovative solutions, both old and new.

A skill so crucial, in life and in class,

In this ability, obstacles we surpass.

Not just for math or science alone,

But in every field, this skill is shown.

A mindset of growth, a can-do attitude,

In this practice, we find fortitude.

What am I, a capability so bold,

In the journey of learning, worth more than gold?

An essential skill, for the challenges we face,

In the quest for solutions, a relentless chase.

Riddle 118

Collaboration and teamwork, in harmony,

Sharing ideas, making decisions collectively.

More than the sum of parts, a synergistic might,

In this method, learning takes flight.

Developing social skills, empathy, and trust,

In this practice, cooperation is a must.

A reflection of the workplace, in future's gaze,

In this approach, teamwork plays.

What am I, a learning strategy so key,

In the curriculum of life, a necessity?

Bringing students together, to collaborate and learn,

In the fabric of education, a vital turn.

Riddle 119

A showcase of knowledge, a skill to refine,

In front of others, your ideas shine.

Organizing thoughts, speaking clear and loud,

In this format, your findings proud.

Not just for the speaker, but the audience too,

A learning experience, offering a view.

A way to communicate, persuade, and inform,

In this practice, confidence is born.

What am I, a task so profound,

In academic and professional grounds found?

A vital skill, in education's quest,

In the realm of communication, among the best.

Riddle 120

The art of oration, in front of a crowd,

To engage, inspire, and make your message loud.

A skill so ancient, yet ever so new,

In this practice, leadership's cue.

Overcoming fear, with each word you convey,

In this form, your confidence on display.

Not just a speech, but a connection true,

In this art, your voice we value.

What am I, a skill so great,

In the world of influence, to articulate?

More than mere talking, a powerful thing,

In the realm of skills, public speaking is king.

Riddle 121

A clash of minds, where arguments soar,

Ideas battle, but respect's at the core.

Not just to win, but understand and probe,

In this arena, the world's globe.

Skills of rhetoric, logic in hand,

Persuading others, to where you stand.

Critical thinking, in real-time, displayed,

In this exchange, foundations are laid.

What am I, an educational tool so keen,

Where voices are heard, and viewpoints seen?

More than competition, a learning spree,

In the world of discourse, I am the key.

Riddle 122

Out in the world, where theory meets land,

Observations and data, collected by hand.

A bridge between classroom and the earth's face,

In this practice, learning finds its place.

Not confined by walls, but open and free,

Exploring environments, where we're meant to be.

A hands-on approach, to knowledge's quest,

In this method, education's at its best.

What am I, an immersive way to learn,

Where the world's complexities, students discern?

A journey outside, beyond the school's gate,

In the field of study, real-world insights await.

Riddle 123

A foray into the professional sphere,

Where learning's applied, career paths clear.

Not just observation, but participation true,

In this experience, skills accrue.

A step from theory, into the real,

Where practical knowledge, students can feel.

A bridge to employment, a valuable link,

In this role, students grow and sync.

What am I, a practical educational stint,

Where futures are formed, in hint after hint?

More than a job, a learning curve steep,

In the world of work, a leap.

Riddle 124

A blend of study and work, in tandem they go,

Alternating between classroom learning and professional show.

Earning while learning, experience gained,

In this program, careers are framed.

Not just for a resume, but skills deep and wide,

In this approach, education's amplified.

A partnership between institutions and firms,

In this model, practical knowledge affirms.

What am I, an integrated path so defined,

Where work and learning are intertwined?

A cooperative education, where students thrive,

In the real world, their skills come alive.

Riddle 125

A journey overseas, to learn and explore,

New cultures, languages, knowledge, and more.

Not just a trip, but an educational quest,

In this experience, growth manifests.

Expanding horizons, beyond home's comfort,

In global classrooms, insights comport.

A transformative chapter, in life's book,

In this adventure, a closer look.

What am I, an opportunity so grand,

Where in foreign lands, learning's hand in hand?

More than travel, an academic stride,

In the global village, we reside.

Riddle 126

Learning in two tongues, from the start,

Enhancing cognition, culture, and heart.

Not just language, but dual knowledge's seed,

In this approach, global citizens we breed.

A curriculum that mirrors, the world's voice,

In this education, diversity's choice.

Building bridges between cultures, so wide,

In this method, understanding's tide.

What am I, a pedagogical blend,

Where two languages, on each other depend?

More than learning, a cultural embrace,

In the world of education, a bilingual base.

Riddle 127

For learners of new tongues, a path so bright,

Mastering English, to read, write, and recite.

Not just words, but a door to the world,

In this program, possibilities unfurled.

A bridge for non-natives, in schools far and wide,

Where language barriers, we seek to override.

A foundation for communication, in global discourse,

In this study, understanding's force.

What am I, an educational course so key,

Where English blooms, for you and me?

More than a subject, a global link,

In the tapestry of languages, a vital ink.

Riddle 128

The ability to read, to write, to comprehend,

In this skill, life's opportunities extend.

Not just for work, but for life's full span,

In this capacity, civilization began.

A fundamental right, in education's creed,

In this knowledge, freedom's seed.

More than letters, a tool for life,

In this skill, empowerment's rife.

What am I, a basic human need,

Where through words, the mind is freed?

More than learning, a societal pillar,

In the realm of growth, a key filler.

Riddle 129

The skill with numbers, to calculate and reason,

In everyday life, through every season.

Not just for math, but decisions informed,

In this ability, daily life is transformed.

A foundation for logic, in finances, time, and space,

In this skill, life's puzzles we face.

More than arithmetic, a critical tool,

In this knowledge, we're not fooled.

What am I, an essential skill so clear,

Where in numbers, solutions appear?

More than counting, a cognitive gift,

In the world of logic, a vital lift.

Riddle 130

A field of study, where innovation's born,

In these disciplines, the future's drawn.

Not just subjects, but a way to think,

In this education, the world's link.

From atoms to algorithms, bridges to bytes,

In this learning, humanity's heights.

A catalyst for progress, in an age so fast,

In this knowledge, our lot is cast.

What am I, an acronym so known,

Where through inquiry, advancements are shown?

More than learning, a global trend,

In the quest for knowledge, we transcend.

Riddle 131

A fusion of fields, where creativity meets logic's embrace,

Adding Arts to STEM, giving innovation a new face.

Science and math, with technology's swift pace,

Engineering's might, and art's grace.

A curriculum that values, the whole mind's space,

Encouraging thinkers, creators, a diverse base.

Not just equations or experiments in a race,

But imagination and design, in education's case.

What am I, a blend so broad,

In learning's spectrum, a harmonious chord?

More than a method, a comprehensive stream,

In the world of education, I am STEAM.

Riddle 132

Guiding lights in the journey of professional quest,

Helping students find paths that suit them best.

Interests, skills, and passions assessed,

In this guidance, futures are dressed.

A bridge between now and dreams so vast,

Ensuring choices made, happiness will last.

Not just advice, but a strategic plan,

In this process, careers began.

What am I, a support so keen,

In the landscape of futures, I'm seen?

More than advice, a critical helping hand,

In the journey of careers, I stand.

Riddle 133

Skills for the workforce, practical and direct,

Education designed, careers to affect.

Hands-on learning, in trades so wide,

In this training, employment's tide.

Not just theory, but application real,

Preparing students, for the job's zeal.

A pathway to employment, clear and defined,

In this system, work and learning intertwined.

What am I, a path so true,

In the world of work, I guide you through?

More than education, a practical insight,

In the landscape of careers, I light.

Riddle 134

A learning model, where experience leads,

Under mentorship, a craft proceeds.

Earning while learning, a trade's secrets shared,

In this journey, skills are prepared.

Not just a student, but a worker in stride,

In this tradition, expertise and growth collide.

A bridge to mastery, in fields so vast,

In this relationship, futures are cast.

What am I, an old path renewed,

In the world of learning, skills accrued?

More than education, a hands-on quest,

In the journey of trades, I'm the test.

Riddle 135

The continuous journey of learning and growth,

Ensuring skills and knowledge, both.

Not stagnant, but evolving in one's career,

In this commitment, excellence is near.

Workshops, seminars, and courses abound,

In this process, new competencies found.

A lifelong commitment to self and field,

In this endeavor, success is sealed.

What am I, a pursuit so grand,

In the realm of careers, I stand?

More than a job, a constant climb,

In the landscape of work, I'm prime.

Riddle 136

Beyond formal years, learning never stops,

Courses, certificates, educational hops.

For personal enrichment or professional need,

In this endeavor, minds continue to feed.

Not just for degrees, but knowledge so wide,

In this learning, growth is implied.

A commitment to lifelong curiosity,

In this path, boundless opportunity.

What am I, a journey so vast,

In the world of knowledge, I'm cast?

More than schooling, an endless quest,

In the realm of learning, I'm the crest.

Riddle 137

For those beyond youth, education's door reopens wide,

Offering learning, life's changes to abide.

From literacy to degrees, a range so vast,

In this system, aspirations are cast.

Not limited by age, but encouraged by desire,

In this education, ambitions aspire.

A second chance, or a new direction to explore,

In this offering, knowledge is more.

What am I, a chance to grow,

In the garden of learning, I sow?

More than a beginning, a lifelong ride,

In the world of education, I guide.

Riddle 138

An ethos of growth, from cradle to grave,

A mindset that knowledge is always a wave.

Not confined to youth, but throughout all life,

In this philosophy, learning cuts like a knife.

A personal commitment, to expand and evolve,

In this journey, problems to solve.

Embracing change, with an open mind,

In this pursuit, endless treasures to find.

What am I, a path so bright,

In the quest for knowledge, an endless flight?

More than education, a way of being,

In the realm of life, I'm freeing.

Riddle 139

A gateway to higher education, accessible and near,

Offering courses, degrees, a career.

A local hub for learning, diverse and wide,

In this institution, communities take pride.

From vocational training to transfer paths clear,

In this college, opportunities dear.

A stepping stone, or a goal in its right,

In this setting, futures bright.

What am I, an educational core,

In the landscape of learning, I open the door?

More than a school, a community's heart,

In the journey of education, a vital part.

Riddle 140

Specializing in skills, trades, and technology's might,

Preparing students for careers, bright.

Hands-on training, with a focus so keen,

In this institution, expertise is seen.

Not just theory, but practice profound,

In this education, professions are found.

A bridge to employment, so direct and sure,

In this path, success is more than a lure.

What am I, a beacon of skill,

In the world of work, I fill?

More than learning, a practical route,

In the landscape of careers, I'm resolute.

Riddle 141

An option distinct, with freedom to design,

Curriculum unique, where new ideas align.

Publicly funded, yet independently run,

In this school, education's tailored fun.

A choice for families, seeking something more,

Where innovation and diversity walk through the door.

Not bound by district, with a charter to guide,

In this institution, learning's a wide ride.

What am I, a school with a special creed,

In the landscape of education, a unique seed?

More than a concept, a reality where learners soar,

In the realm of possibilities, I open the door.

Riddle 142

Funded by fees, and donations, not state,

In this setting, education can be great.

Selective in admissions, with a mission clear,

In this school, a community dear.

Often with a focus, religious or pure,

In academic pursuits, results are sure.

Smaller classes, attention so keen,

In this environment, potential is seen.

What am I, an institution with choice,

In the world of education, a distinct voice?

More than a school, a place of distinct measure,

In the quest for knowledge, a treasure.

Riddle 143

Open to all, with funding from the state,

In this school, education's plate.

A cornerstone of democracy, free to attend,

In this system, on which many depend.

Reflecting society, diverse and broad,

In these classrooms, future's chord.

A commitment to educate every child,

In this mission, possibilities compiled.

What am I, a foundation so strong,

In the tapestry of learning, where all belong?

More than a building, a community's core,

In the journey of education, an open door.

Riddle 144

A home away from home, where students reside,

In this setting, education and life collide.

Not just for learning, but living together,

In this institution, bonds form forever.

Discipline, structure, and routines define,

In this school, students shine.

A comprehensive experience, day and night,

In this journey, growth in every sight.

What am I, a place of learning so whole,

In the realm of education, a nurturing role?

More than a school, a life's chapter so bold,

In the story of youth, my tale is told.

Riddle 145

Education at home, where parents guide the way,

In this method, tailored learning each day.

Flexible and personal, adapting to each child,

In this setting, imaginations run wild.

Not confined by walls, or a bell's toll,

In this system, learning's in control.

A choice for many, for reasons so vast,

In this approach, education's cast.

What am I, a path less taken, yet true,

In the world of learning, a personal view?

More than an option, a lifestyle indeed,

In the journey of education, a different seed.

Riddle 146

A child-centered approach, where learners lead,

In this environment, curiosity's feed.

Hands-on learning, with materials designed,

In this philosophy, development's intertwined.

Respect, independence, a community feel,

In this setting, education's real.

A global movement, with a vision so clear,

In this method, the child's sphere.

What am I, an educational creed,

Where in each child, potential's freed?

More than a method, a holistic approach,

In the landscape of learning, a global broach.

Riddle 147

An approach holistic, arts and academics combined,

In this education, creativity and cognition entwined.

Rhythms of learning, respecting child's pace,

In this philosophy, growth's grace.

Imagination, critical thinking, both revered,

In this setting, future pioneers are geared.

A curriculum rich, with nature and myth,

In this school, a broad bandwidth.

What am I, a path with roots deep,

In the forest of education, a leap?

More than teaching, a way to see the world,

In the garden of learning, my flag's unfurled.

Riddle 148

Born from a town, where children's voices reign,

In this philosophy, learning's a gain.

Project-based, collaborative, with respect so vast,

In this environment, education's cast.

A reflection of the community, with families in tow,

In this method, children's potentials grow.

Documentation of learning, a narrative shared,

In this approach, every detail cared.

What am I, an educational view,

Where through exploration, insights accrue?

More than a system, a dialogue with the young,

In the world of pedagogy, my praises sung.

Riddle 149

A division of education, geographic in span,

Overseeing schools, to a strategic plan.

Administration of resources, policies, and more,

In this jurisdiction, education's core.

Responsible for the quality, ensuring standards met,

In this structure, goals are set.

A community's educational framework, indeed,

In this organization, students' needs lead.

What am I, an area defined,

In the landscape of education, aligned?

More than a boundary, a governance so vital,

In the realm of schooling, a title.

Riddle 150

Guidelines and rules, shaping the way,

How learning's conducted, day by day.

Affecting everyone, from student to teacher,

In this framework, education's feature.

Not just laws, but a vision so broad,

In this document, future's nod.

Crafting the path, for systems so vast,

In this policy, education's cast.

What am I, a blueprint so grand,

In the world of learning, I stand?

More than guidelines, a mission's voice,

In the journey of education, a choice.

Riddle 151

A principle of fairness, where each learner's needs are met,

Not just equality, but justice in the set.

Tailoring resources, so all can succeed,

In this pursuit, every student we heed.

Recognizing differences, yet providing a chance,

For every background, circumstance.

A goal so noble, in education's quest,

Ensuring all are given their best.

What am I, a cause so pure,

In the realm of learning, the cure?

More than a concept, a mission so right,

In the world of education, I fight.

Riddle 152

A welcoming classroom, where diversity's embraced,

Differences celebrated, not erased.

Every student's part of the collective heart,

In this approach, everyone has a part.

Barriers removed, so learning's accessible,

In this setting, success is possible.

A reflection of society, in its broadest sense,

In this methodology, confidence commences.

What am I, a model so broad,

Where all learners are applauded by the squad?

More than a strategy, a culture, a vision,

In the world of education, my mission.

Riddle 153

Navigating the web, understanding its flow,

Critical thinking online, in this knowledge we grow.

Not just surfing, but engaging with a critical mind,

In this skill, the truth we find.

Creating content, ethically and wise,

In this era, digital literacy rises.

A necessity in today's connected age,

In this domain, we engage.

What am I, a skill so key,

In the digital world, the way to see?

More than using technology, a comprehensive guide,

In the information age, I'm your ride.

Riddle 154

Analyzing messages, in every form they come,

Understanding bias, where they're from.

A skill to discern, critique, and create,

In this literacy, we navigate.

Not just passive consumers, but active participants,

In this knowledge, our vigilance.

Empowered to question, to understand, to express,

In this field, we assess.

What am I, an essential ability,

In the age of information, the key to see clearly?

More than reading, a critical interaction,

In the world of media, I'm the action.

Riddle 155

Understanding rights, responsibilities, and roles,

In this learning, democracy's goals.

Not just the structure of government and law,

But active participation, without flaw.

Developing informed, engaged citizens,

In this study, society's linchpins.

A foundation for democracy, vibrant and strong,

In this curriculum, we belong.

What am I, a subject so vital,

In the realm of governance, my title?

More than knowledge, an engagement spree,

In the fabric of society, I'm key.

Riddle 156

Learning about the planet, our impact, and care,

In this study, awareness we share.

Not just science, but a way to live,

In this education, respect we give.

Sustainability, conservation, and more,

In this learning, the Earth we adore.

Empowering students to make a difference,

In this field, with persistence.

What am I, a lesson so grand,

In the stewardship of the land?

More than a subject, a lifelong quest,

In the care of Earth, I'm the test.

Riddle 157

Promoting wellness, understanding disease,

In this curriculum, ease and unease.

Not just physical, but mental well-being too,

In this education, a comprehensive view.

Teaching about nutrition, exercise, and rest,

In this learning, to live our best.

A vital component of every student's day,

In this domain, we find our way.

What am I, a subject so key,

In the journey of life, the way to be?

More than instruction, a foundation for health,

In the world of education, my wealth.

Riddle 158

The ability to move, with competence and joy,

In this skill, life's employ.

Not just sports, but daily activities too,

In this literacy, through and through.

Confidence in motion, coordination, and play,

In this learning, we sway.

A fundamental for health, throughout life's span,

In this endeavor, we can.

What am I, a concept so broad,

In the realm of wellness, not just applaud?

More than fitness, a way of life,

In the tapestry of health, I'm rife.

Riddle 159

Managing money, understanding savings, and debt,

In this knowledge, a safety net.

Not just numbers, but a way to thrive,

In this literacy, we derive.

Budgeting, investing, and planning for the future,

In this education, no suture.

A skill so crucial, in today's economy,

In this learning, autonomy.

What am I, a need so clear,

In the world of finance, I steer?

More than math, a life skill indeed,

In the journey of adulthood, I lead.

Riddle 160

A curriculum that reflects the world's diverse face,

In this learning, every culture has a place.

Not just tolerance, but appreciation and respect,

In this education, aspects we inspect.

Teaching about histories, languages, and beliefs,

In this study, understanding reliefs.

Preparing students for a global society,

In this approach, a variety of propriety.

What am I, an educational philosophy so wide,

In the realm of diversity, I guide?

More than a subject, a way to embrace,

In the world of learning, every race.

Riddle 161

A field that explores, beyond mere binary bounds,

Where identity, culture, and society surrounds.

Not just about women or men, but all in between,

In this study, the spectrum's seen.

Challenging norms, questioning roles so defined,

In this discipline, new understandings we find.

Intersecting with race, class, and more,

In this inquiry, perspectives soar.

What am I, a subject so vast,

In the realm of academia, I'm cast?

More than a course, a critical lens,

In the tapestry of knowledge, where inquiry commences.

Riddle 162

A guide in the realm where classrooms extend,

Beyond walls, in virtual spaces blend.

Ensuring that learners, though far, stay connected,

In this role, paths are directed.

Technology and education, in harmony they dance,

In this person's hands, learning's advance.

A bridge between students and digital courseware,

In this position, care and prepare.

What am I, a facilitator so key,

In the world of online education, I oversee?

More than a role, a vital link,

In the journey of distance learning, I sync.

Riddle 163

An expert in learning, with wisdom to lend,

Advising schools, from start to end.

Curriculum, policy, and strategy in their grasp,

In this profession, solutions they clasp.

Not just a guide, but a visionary true,

In this role, education's view.

Improving outcomes, enhancing the experience,

In this consultancy, excellence's adherence.

What am I, a professional so wise,

In the landscape of education, my advice rises?

More than a counselor, an architect of learning's flow,

In the realm of schooling, I help grow.

Riddle 164

A mentor for students, on their educational path,

Guiding courses, careers, and aftermath.

Helping navigate, through choices so wide,

In this role, alongside they stride.

Not just for schedules, but dreams to chase,

In this advisor, trust and embrace.

A beacon through the academic maze,

In this person, guidance and praise.

What am I, a guide so keen,

In the world of academia, often seen?

More than a planner, a supporter at heart,

In the journey of education, a vital part.

Riddle 165

A healer of minds, in the educational sphere,

Supporting students, to learn without fear.

Emotional, social, and academic strife,

In this role, they aid life.

Not just a counselor, but a researcher too,

In this profession, insights accrue.

Creating environments, where all can thrive,

In this work, students' potentials arrive.

What am I, a caretaker so profound,

In the landscape of learning, where support is found?

More than a therapist, an educational ally,

In the realm of schooling, I apply.

Riddle 166

The goals of education, clearly defined,

What students will know, do, and find.

Beyond mere objectives, outcomes are broad,

In this concept, learning's accord.

Assessing not just the process, but the end,

In this principle, on which we depend.

Guiding curriculum, teaching, and more,

In this outcome, knowledge's core.

What am I, an aim so clear,

In the process of education, I steer?

More than a target, a comprehensive view,

In the journey of learning, I'm true.

Riddle 167

A model where mastery, not time, leads the way,

In this approach, skills display.

Not just about passing, but truly understanding,

In this system, no student is left standing.

Each at their pace, moving as they achieve,

In this framework, success they retrieve.

Skills and knowledge, the true measure,

In this method, learning's treasure.

What am I, a paradigm shift,

In the world of education, I uplift?

More than a method, a revolution in learning,

In the quest for knowledge, I'm yearning.

Riddle 168

Together in time, though not in space,

In this mode, learning's embrace.

Live interactions, digital or face-to-face,

In this setting, community's grace.

A real-time exchange, of ideas so wide,

In this format, together we ride.

Not isolated, but connected and direct,

In this learning, respect and reflect.

What am I, a simultaneous flow,

In the world of education, together we grow?

More than a method, a dynamic exchange,

In the landscape of learning, I range.

Riddle 169

A self-paced journey, through digital lands,

In this approach, learning expands.

Videos, readings, forums to explore,

In this method, flexibility's core.

Not bound by time, or a single place,

In this format, learning's own pace.

A way to study, that's flexible and broad,

In this model, knowledge's accord.

What am I, a path so free,

In the realm of online education, I be?

More than a choice, an opportunity vast,

In the world of learning, I'm cast.

Riddle 170

A commitment to fairness, in schools and class,

Ensuring all students have the chance to pass.

Not just equality, but equity in deed,

In this goal, every learner's need.

Addressing disparities, resources aligned,

In this pursuit, justice we find.

A foundation for democracy, opportunity's key,

In this concept, all are free to be.

What am I, a principle so just,

In the world of education, in me, you trust?

More than a policy, a moral quest,

In the journey towards fairness, I'm the test.

Riddle 171

In halls and classrooms, a shield I stand,

Against the tide of harm that's planned.

Teaching respect, empathy, and care,

In my lessons, fairness is laid bare.

Not just reactive, but proactive too,

Creating environments respectful and true.

A crusade against the hurt, the tease, the scorn,

In my embrace, safer spaces are born.

What am I, a campaign so bold,

Against the bullying, in schools, old and cold?

More than a policy, a culture, a norm,

In the fight for kindness, I form.

Riddle 172

A bond between learners, guidance shared,

Experience and wisdom, openly bared.

Not just a tutor, but a friend in the quest,

In my program, support is expressed.

Older or wiser, or just a step ahead,

In my structure, confidence is spread.

A bridge between novices and the known,

In my guidance, seeds of success are sown.

What am I, a connection so key,

In the journey of learning, peer to peer, you see?

More than assistance, a passage of insight,

In the realm of education, a guiding light.

Riddle 173

The focus shifts, from teacher to the taught,

Where learners' needs, aspirations, and thoughts are sought.

Not just a vessel to be filled, but a flame to light,

In my philosophy, students' curiosity takes flight.

Empowerment, agency, a voice in the crowd,

In my approach, inquiry is allowed.

A shift in the paradigm, where learners lead,

In my framework, their ambitions feed.

What am I, a method so true,

Where education's gaze on the student, anew?

More than a technique, a transformative creed,

In the landscape of learning, student needs lead.

Riddle 174

Tailored teaching, to each unique mind,

Acknowledging that no two learners are quite aligned.

Varied in approach, in pace, and in style,

In my strategy, each student can smile.

Not just one path, but many to explore,

In my application, learning's not a chore.

A mosaic of methodologies, so diverse and wide,

In my practice, inclusivity is implied.

What am I, an educational art,

Where teaching's tailored, right from the start?

More than a policy, a pedagogical blend,

In the journey of learning, adaptiveness I send.

Riddle 175

A framework so broad, for all to access,

Removing barriers, in education's progress.

Multiple means of engagement, representation, action, and expression,

In my design, learning's a confession.

Not just for some, but for every learner's right,

In my structure, education's light.

A guide to teaching, that's inclusive and fair,

In my methodology, diversity's care.

What am I, a blueprint so vast,

In the realm of education, inclusively cast?

More than a concept, a foundational guide,

In the architecture of learning, I preside.

Riddle 176

Education as a path to liberation, not just skill,

Questioning power, a will to instill.

Not just absorbing, but transforming the world,

In my teachings, critical consciousness unfurled.

Empowering learners, to think and to act,

In my philosophy, society's pact.

A dialogue between teacher and student, engaged,

In my practice, critical minds are staged.

What am I, a pedagogy so deep,

Where education's more than a leap?

More than teaching, a revolutionary creed,

In the quest for justice, my seed.

Riddle 177

Learning through doing, a task that's real,

Engagement and inquiry, in my appeal.

Not just a lesson, but a journey to explore,

In my approach, competencies galore.

Collaboration, investigation, synthesis, and more,

In my application, learning's core.

A bridge between theory and the practical world,

In my methodology, knowledge unfurled.

What am I, an instructional model so grand,

Where through projects, insights land?

More than an activity, a pedagogical scheme,

In the landscape of learning, a practical dream.

Riddle 178

A blend of service, community, and education,

In my model, civic participation's foundation.

Learning through helping, a reciprocal deed,

In my practice, empathy and understanding seed.

Not just volunteerism, but integrated with course goals,

In my framework, character and competence rolls.

Reflecting on the experience, its impact so wide,

In my structure, personal and societal pride.

What am I, a method so key,

Where learning and service agree?

More than a program, a transformative action,

In the curriculum of life, a fraction.

Riddle 179

Learning by experiencing, the world as a class,

Not just theories, but realities amass.

Reflection, critical analysis, and synthesis in tow,

In my cycle, knowledge and skills grow.

Direct engagement with the subject at hand,

In my domain, active learning's stand.

A holistic approach, involving the learner's being,

In my philosophy, seeing is freeing.

What am I, an approach so vast,

Where learning's anchored in experiences cast?

More than a method, a way to perceive,

In the journey of education, to achieve.

Riddle 180

Questions lead the way, in my domain,

Curiosity's reign, in this terrain.

Not just answers provided, but discovered and sought,

In my practice, critical thinking's taught.

A student-led approach, where exploration's key,

In my landscape, learning's free.

Encouraging investigation, dialogue, and debate,

In my methodology, inquiry's the gate.

What am I, a pedagogical path,

Where questioning drives the learning's wrath?

More than a technique, an investigative spree,

In the world of education, curiosity's key.

Riddle 181

A guidepost for knowledge, what we aim to achieve,

Clear targets for learners, in what they conceive.

Not just goals, but the outcomes we expect,

In my framework, success we detect.

Specific and measurable, achievable, and relevant,

In my design, education's element.

Guiding teaching and assessment, hand in hand,

In my presence, learning's plan stands grand.

What am I, a beacon so bright,

In the journey of education, guiding light?

More than intentions, a path so clear,

In the realm of learning, I steer.

Riddle 182

A tool for assessment, detailed and defined,

Criteria and standards, in me, you'll find.

Not just subjective, but structured and fair,

In my application, clarity's air.

Guiding students and teachers, alike in their quest,

In my use, understanding's test.

Feedback and grading, transparent and true,

In my structure, improvement's cue.

What am I, a framework so key,

In the world of evaluation, I decree?

More than a guide, a measure precise,

In the landscape of learning, my advice.

Riddle 183

A stamp of approval, quality assured,

Standards met, by institutions secured.

Not just a label, but a mark of trust,

In my certification, excellence is a must.

Recognition by authorities, in education's field,

In my status, institutions' fate is sealed.

A promise of credibility, to those who inquire,

In my presence, aspirations soar higher.

What am I, a designation so grand,

In the realm of education, a quality brand?

More than validation, a commitment shown,

In the world of academia, respectably known.

Riddle 184

Learning materials, freely accessed and shared,

Knowledge's bounty, generously spared.

Not just content, but tools and practices, too,

In my universe, education's view.

Removing barriers, to information's flow,

In my adoption, understanding grows.

A revolution in resources, for all to use,

In my essence, the open web's muse.

What am I, a resource so free,

In the landscape of learning, the key?

More than materials, an open door,

In the realm of education, I'm the core.

Riddle 185

A gift of learning, financial support bestowed,

For the diligent, a path less owed.

Not just assistance, but recognition of merit,

In my grant, dreams inherit.

Easing the burden, of education's cost,

In my presence, fewer dreams are lost.

A bridge to opportunities, for those who strive,

In my offering, aspirations come alive.

What am I, a boon so bright,

In the journey of scholars, a guiding light?

More than aid, an honor to hold,

In the realm of academia, a story told.

Riddle 186

The growth of thinking, reasoning, and knowing,

In my essence, minds ever-growing.

Not just learning, but how we understand,

In my study, intellect's expand.

Stages and theories, Piaget to the fore,

In my domain, knowledge's lore.

The framework of mental processes, intricate and vast,

In my presence, learning's cast.

What am I, a concept so deep,

In the development of minds, a leap?

More than mere thought, a developmental ride,

In the realm of psychology, I preside.

Riddle 187

A strategy to modify, actions deemed askew,

In my application, change ensues.

Not just correction, but guidance and support,

In my approach, positive behavior's court.

From classrooms to therapy, my methods are applied,

In my practice, better outcomes spied.

A systematic approach, to alter what's seen,

In my execution, transformation's keen.

What am I, a method so clear,

In the landscape of behavior, I steer?

More than change, a structured plan,

In the realm of development, I span.

Riddle 188

The heart of education, beyond the mind's reach,

Empathy, self-awareness, skills we teach.

Not just academic, but life's essential part,

In my core, understanding the heart.

Building relationships, managing emotions, and more,

In my embrace, character's core.

A foundation for well-being, for life's every test,

In my practice, learners are best.

What am I, a curriculum so whole,

In the schooling of life, I play a role?

More than lessons, a holistic view,

In the journey of growth, I renew.

Riddle 189

The belief in potential, that abilities can expand,

In my philosophy, efforts command.

Not fixed or static, but malleable and free,

In my presence, possibilities be.

Challenges embraced, failures seen as a start,

In my thinking, resilience's heart.

A shift from "can't" to "not yet," in time,

In my view, learning's prime.

What am I, a mindset so bright,

In the face of obstacles, a guiding light?

More than attitude, a transformative belief,

In the realm of achievement, I am chief.

Riddle 190

Navigating the web, with ethics in hand,

In my code, respect and understand.

Not just using, but contributing right,

In my doctrine, online etiquette's light.

Safety, privacy, and interaction online,

In my teachings, boundaries define.

A responsible member of the digital age,

In my practice, wisdom's page.

What am I, a concept so key,

In the world connected, how to be?

More than behavior, an educated stance,

In the digital realm, my advance.

Riddle 191

A set of rules, a guiding light,

In halls of learning, keeping standards tight.

Not just words, but actions too,

In my presence, respect's in view.

A framework for behavior, for all to see,

In my bounds, how we agree to be.

Promoting safety, respect, and fairness,

In my realm, addressing carelessness.

What am I, a document so clear,

In the community of education, I steer?

More than guidance, a moral plea,

In the culture of academia, I decree.

Riddle 192

The cornerstone of scholarship, honest and true,

In research, writing, and review.

Not just avoiding cheating, but in citations bright,

In my honor, intellectual fights.

A commitment to truth, in all that's done,

In my spirit, accolades are won.

Ethical standards, in learning and tests,

In my adherence, trust manifests.

What am I, a principle so revered,

In the halls of knowledge, clearly steered?

More than a rule, a culture deep,

In the landscape of learning, a pact we keep.

Riddle 193

The theft of ideas, not just mere words,

In my shadow, integrity's blurred.

Not just copy and paste, but the theft of thought,

In my avoidance, honesty's sought.

A violation grave, in academic spheres,

In my wake, consequences and fears.

Teaching the value of originality,

In my lesson, creativity's reality.

What am I, a breach so stark,

In the realm of scholarship, missing the mark?

More than an error, a serious misdeed,

In the quest for knowledge, a warning to heed.

Riddle 194

A pledge of honesty, a vow so true,

In academia, a guide through and through.

Not just a promise, but a lifestyle's creed,

In my observance, integrity's seed.

A commitment by students, to act with respect,

In my culture, trust we protect.

Self-regulation, a community's bond,

In my spirit, ethics correspond.

What am I, an oath so grand,

In the halls of education, where we stand?

More than words, a collective embrace,

In the pursuit of knowledge, a noble base.

Riddle 195

Diverse learners, each unique,

In my care, their strengths we seek.

Not just a label, but a spectrum wide,

In my understanding, support provided.

Tailored approaches, accommodations right,

In my world, every learner's plight.

A commitment to inclusion, equity in deed,

In my embrace, potential freed.

What am I, a term so broad,

In the landscape of learning, a supportive nod?

More than a category, a personalized view,

In the realm of education, a commitment true.

Riddle 196

Tools that assist, making learning accessible,

In my use, barriers are addressable.

Not just software, but devices too,

In my arsenal, independence we pursue.

Customizing experiences, for needs so varied,

In my application, no one's carried.

Enabling participation, in education's race,

In my presence, equality's base.

What am I, a technological aid,

In the journey of learning, foundations laid?

More than gadgets, an empowering stream,

In the realm of special needs, a dream.

Riddle 197

Actions tailored, to support and guide,

In my planning, needs identified.

Not just remediation, but enrichment too,

In my application, growth in view.

Targeted teaching, behavioral supports,

In my arsenal, success of sorts.

A bridge over gaps, a push to exceed,

In my execution, achievement's seed.

What am I, a methodical approach,

In the field of education, progress's coach?

More than tactics, a comprehensive plan,

In the landscape of learning, a supportive van.

Riddle 198

A catch-up course, for those behind,

In my classrooms, the basics they find.

Not just a review, but a foundation's build,

In my presence, gaps are filled.

Addressing challenges, in reading, math, and more,

In my teaching, skills restore.

A step towards equality, in education's quest,

In my structure, success is addressed.

What am I, a program so key,

In the journey of learners, a supportive sea?

More than correction, a new start,

In the realm of education, a vital part.

Riddle 199

For those who soar, beyond the norm,

In my care, their talents transform.

Not just acceleration, but depth and complexity,

In my planning, creativity's intensity.

Enrichment, differentiation, in stride,

In my domain, brilliance doesn't hide.

A nurturing of potential, so bright and keen,

In my embrace, the future's seen.

What am I, a tailored approach,

In the education landscape, a beacon's torch?

More than a program, an acknowledgment wide,

In the realm of learning, where talents abide.

Riddle 200

A movement for change, in systems set,

In my wave, improvements we get.

Not just policy, but practice and thought,

In my journey, better futures sought.

Addressing equity, quality, innovation too,

In my mission, perspectives anew.

A shift towards better, for every learner's right,

In my cause, education's light.

What am I, a pursuit so vast,

In the world of learning, my cast?

More than adjustments, a transformative creed,

In the landscape of education, progress's seed.

Riddle 201

In classrooms and beyond, I'm the guide to the real,

Teaching how to cook, budget, and deal.

Not just academics, but the art of living,

In my lessons, practical wisdom I'm giving.

Communication, empathy, and self-care in my fold,

For life's challenges, in you, I mold.

A curriculum of existence, broad and true,

In my embrace, life's hues you view.

What am I, a foundation so vast,

In the journey of life, lessons to last?

More than a subject, a preparation for all,

In the realm of growth, I stand tall.

Riddle 202

Hands-on learning, with a future in sight,

In my classrooms, skills take flight.

Not just theory, but the practical too,

In my guidance, careers pursue.

From healthcare to tech, trades galore,

In my training, opportunities door.

A bridge to employment, education aligned,

In my pathway, success you'll find.

What am I, education with a direct aim,

In the landscape of work, I claim?

More than learning, a career's start,

In the journey of skill, I'm a part.

Riddle 203

Earn and learn, a balance so fine,

In my structure, work and education intertwine.

Financial aid that requires your time,

In my program, experience and income climb.

Not just a job, but a part of your growth,

In my design, a pledge to both.

A way to manage college expenses, smart,

In my offer, education's heart.

What am I, a dual role to play,

In the realm of academia, a way?

More than employment, a support to learn,

In the journey of education, my turn.

Riddle 204

High school and college, simultaneously,

In my program, credits accrue freely.

Not just for the advanced, but all who dare,

In my opportunity, academic care.

A head start on higher education's path,

In my course, lessening future math.

Saving time and money, credits in hand,

In my scheme, ahead you stand.

What am I, a bridge so keen,

In the journey of learning, seen?

More than a class, an acceleration's gate,

In the realm of education, I integrate.

Riddle 205

A blend of adolescence and higher learning's quest,

In my halls, students are put to the test.

Not just a diploma, but a degree in sight,

In my innovation, future's bright.

Challenging the norms, breaking the mold,

In my embrace, young scholars bold.

A head start on the journey, before the rest,

In my program, students are blessed.

What am I, an institution so rare,

In the landscape of education, I dare?

More than a school, a transformative chance,

In the realm of growth, I enhance.

Riddle 206

A pause in the academic race,

In my time, the world you embrace.

Not just a break, but a journey of soul,

In my span, discovery's role.

Travel, volunteer, or work to find,

In my period, yourself unbind.

A chance to grow, learn, and prepare,

In my offer, life's affair.

What am I, a hiatus so bold,

In the journey of life, stories told?

More than a gap, a formative year,

In the realm of experience, I endear.

Riddle 207

A collection of works, showing what you've done,

In my compilation, skills and victories won.

Not just tests, but creations and reflections,

In my review, directions' detections.

A holistic view of your learning path,

In my pages, your academic craft.

Demonstrating growth, projects, and skill,

In my narrative, your potential's thrill.

What am I, a record so diverse,

In the evaluation of education, I converse?

More than a grade, a story complete,

In the realm of achievement, I'm discrete.

Riddle 208

A formal record, of courses and grades,

In my document, your academic parades.

Not just a paper, but a history told,

In my lines, your efforts bold.

Every class, every score, in detail,

In my ledger, your educational trail.

A key to the future, colleges inspect,

In my record, your intellect reflect.

What am I, an academic summary,

In the journey of learning, your story?

More than a list, a credential's source,

In the realm of education, I'm a course.

Riddle 209

A recognition of excellence, grades so high,

In my honor, academic spirits fly.

Not just a title, but a mark of distinction,

In my list, dedication's inscription.

For those who excel, semester by term,

In my mention, their achievements affirm.

A motivation for students, to strive and achieve,

In my accolade, their efforts receive.

What am I, an honor so grand,

In the landscape of academia, a commendable stand?

More than an award, a testament true,

In the realm of success, a view.

Riddle 210

A celebration of endings and beginnings anew,

In my ceremony, achievements we review.

Not just a goodbye, but a welcome forward,

In my occasion, futures are authored.

Caps thrown high, in joy and in pride,

In my moment, transitions coincide.

A threshold crossed, with diplomas in hand,

In my event, graduates stand.

What am I, a milestone so bright,

In the journey of education, a height?

More than a ceremony, life's new stage,

In the realm of achievements, my page.

Riddle 211

A gathering of minds, both new and old,

Where tales of future and past are told.

Not just a meeting, but a ceremony grand,

In my moment, academia stands hand in hand.

The beginning of journeys, with wisdom and cheer,

In my assembly, the academic year we revere.

A celebration of learning, community's embrace,

In my tradition, education's grace.

What am I, a commencement of sorts,

In the realm of scholars, a supportive fort?

More than an event, a collective cheer,

In the cycle of study, I appear.

Riddle 212

Blueprints of courses, outlines so clear,

In my pages, objectives appear.

Not just a document, but a contract too,

In my guidance, the semester's view.

Expectations set, readings and dates defined,

In my structure, the academic mind's refined.

A roadmap for learning, for both teacher and student,

In my preparation, success is prudent.

What am I, a guide at the start,

In the journey of education, playing my part?

More than a plan, a promise to keep,

In the landscape of learning, I leap.

Riddle 213

A cycle of learning, seasons in turn,

In my passage, knowledge we earn.

Not just a span of time, but a rhythm so deep,

In my bounds, promises to keep.

From fall to summer, a journey through pages,

In my chapters, wisdom ages.

A division of semesters, or terms to adhere,

In my calendar, education's sphere.

What am I, a timeframe so bound,

In the realm of academia, where I'm found?

More than months, a structured quest,

In the pursuit of knowledge, I vest.

Riddle 214

Dividing the year, into thirds so neat,

In my segment, challenges and achievements meet.

Not just a portion, but a pace to sustain,

In my duration, learning's gain.

A system that offers, a faster pace,

In my structure, a lively race.

Each part distinct, with goals to achieve,

In my cycle, progress we weave.

What am I, a term so defined,

In the calendar of learning, intertwined?

More than a period, a frequent start,

In the narrative of education, my part.

Riddle 215

A division of the year, into four distinct parts,

In my system, new beginnings and restarts.

Not just a slice, but a rapid flow,

In my sequence, knowledge grows.

Each quarter brings, its own set of classes,

In my rhythm, time swiftly passes.

A model for those, who seek more starts,

In my framework, education imparts.

What am I, a fraction so keen,

In the academic cycle, often seen?

More than a segment, a dynamic chart,

In the realm of study, a crucial part.

Riddle 216

A leader in academia, with a vision so broad,

In my role, faculties I laud.

Not just an administrator, but a guide so wise,

In my decisions, the academic standard lies.

Overseeing programs, faculty, and more,

In my guardianship, education's core.

A pillar of the institution, with a steady hand,

In my stewardship, quality stands.

What am I, an office of esteem,

In the hierarchy of education, a supreme?

More than a title, a responsibility grand,

In the world of learning, I command.

Riddle 217

The chief academic officer, in the university's trust,

In my oversight, academic policies adjust.

Not just a position, but a leadership so prime,

In my care, excellence over time.

Curriculum, research, and faculty affairs,

In my realm, the academic welfare flares.

A bridge between the president and the academic scene,

In my balance, integrity's keen.

What am I, a role so pivotal,

In the structure of academia, critical?

More than an administrator, a vision's host,

In the realm of education, I am the provost.

Riddle 218

A warning signal, for those off track,

In my phase, a chance to come back.

Not just a penalty, but a call to rise,

In my period, improvement's prize.

A time to reflect, reassess, and renew,

In my span, support to see you through.

Guidance and resources, to help you succeed,

In my measure, a wake-up indeed.

What am I, a moment so stark,

In the journey of learning, a marker, a mark?

More than a status, an opportunity clear,

In the realm of academia, to steer.

Riddle 219

A hub of assistance, where knowledge is shared,

In my space, no question is spared.

Not just for the struggling, but for all who seek,

In my service, the answers you peek.

A supplement to lectures, a personalized touch,

In my domain, progress is such.

From math to science, writing, and more,

In my rooms, confidence is restored.

What am I, a resource so bright,

In the landscape of education, a guiding light?

More than help, a community of support,

In the realm of learning, a comforting port.

Riddle 220

A sanctuary for writers, of essays and reports,

In my quarters, constructive feedback of sorts.

Not just for the troubled, but for those who aspire,

In my counsel, skills transpire.

Crafting arguments, structure, and style,

In my guidance, writing's worthwhile.

A place to refine, to edit and review,

In my assistance, your voice anew.

What am I, a workshop so keen,

In the realm of expression, often seen?

More than a service, an educational art,

In the journey of writing, I impart.

Riddle 221

A place of inquiry, where theories come to life,

In my bounds, curiosity and innovation are rife.

Not just a room, but a world of discovery and test,

In my space, young minds are put to their best.

From circuits to cells, equations to stars,

In my domain, the future's not far.

Hands-on learning, experiments abound,

In my atmosphere, solutions are found.

What am I, a hub of science and more,

In the realm of education, an exploratory shore?

More than a classroom, a catalyst for thought,

In the landscape of STEM, battles are fought.

Riddle 222

A realm where tongues from around the globe meet,

In my air, learning's sweet.

Not just a place, but a portal to the world,

In my embrace, communication's unfurled.

With headphones and mics, technology at play,

In my sessions, languages sway.

A bridge to understanding, cultures, and speech,

In my care, global connections we reach.

What am I, a room of voices and sounds,

In the journey of learning, where diversity abounds?

More than a lab, a place of linguistic blend,

In the quest for fluency, I'm a friend.

Riddle 223

A chamber of knowledge, where ideas are broadcast,

In my seats, students are amassed.

Not just a space, but a vessel of learning's voyage,

In my expanse, wisdom's storage.

Where one speaks, and many listen,

In my confines, thoughts glisten.

A traditional scene, of education's past and present,

In my presence, lectures are pleasant.

What am I, a hall so vast,

In the landscape of academia, firmly cast?

More than a room, a theater of the mind,

In the pursuit of knowledge, a find.

Riddle 224

A heart of campus life, where students find their kin,

In my halls, community begins.

Not just a building, but a home for all to share,

In my embrace, you're free of care.

From clubs to councils, cafes to lounges,

In my quarters, culture bounces.

A center of activity, for leisure and for voice,

In my domain, students rejoice.

What am I, a hub of student zest,

In the realm of education, a communal nest?

More than a place, a gathering of spirit and fun,

In the journey of college, I'm the sun.

Riddle 225

A residence of learners, in close quarters they stay,

In my rooms, life unfolds in a collegiate way.

Not just a bed, but a space of growth and bond,

In my walls, friendships are fond.

The backdrop of memories, late-night talks, and more,

In my existence, experiences store.

A step from home, into independence's embrace,

In my structure, young lives interlace.

What am I, a home away from home, so dear,

In the landscape of learning, students' near?

More than a building, a part of college lore,

In the realm of academia, I'm the core.

Riddle 226

The keeper of records, where courses and grades reside,

In my care, academic histories are applied.

Not just an office, but the heart of the school's order,

In my guardianship, boundaries are broader.

Enrollment, transcripts, and certification, too,

In my domain, educational journeys ensue.

A pivotal role, in the fabric of education's weave,

In my charge, integrity we achieve.

What am I, an administrative guide,

In the infrastructure of learning, wide?

More than a role, a steward of the academic quest,

In the journey of students, I invest.

Riddle 227

The formal entry, into an institution's fold,

In my process, futures bold.

Not just registration, but a rite of passage clear,

In my moment, academic careers appear.

A beginning of a journey, in higher education's land,

In my step, aspirations grand.

A commitment made, to learn, to grow, to strive,

In my embrace, ambitions thrive.

What am I, an initiation so grand,

In the realm of academia, a welcoming hand?

More than an act, a milestone so bright,

In the landscape of learning, a flight.

Riddle 228

A doorway to exploration, where institutions invite,

In my event, futures bright.

Not just a tour, but a showcase of potential's space,

In my hours, opportunities face.

Families and students wander, questions in tow,

In my setting, information's flow.

A glimpse into what might be, in education's halls,

In my time, the future calls.

What am I, an invitation so wide,

In the journey of selection, a guide?

More than a visit, a preview of what's in store,

In the realm of education, an open door.

Riddle 229

A meeting of minds, for the student's sake,

In my dialogue, progress we make.

Not just a talk, but a partnership's start,

In my exchange, insights impart.

Concerns and achievements, openly discussed,

In my conversation, trust is a must.

A bridge between home and school, for growth's aim,

In my session, understanding's claim.

What am I, a collaborative meet,

In the landscape of learning, a connection sweet?

More than a conference, a union of care,

In the journey of education, a share.

Riddle 230

A crusade for kindness, where respect is sown,

In my mission, safety's grown.

Not just a policy, but a culture's embrace,

In my effort, dignity's base.

Education, intervention, standing side by side,

In my plan, courage and love abide.

Creating environments where all can thrive,

In my goal, compassion's alive.

What am I, a movement so bold,

In the realm of well-being, a fold?

More than a campaign, a societal rendition,

In the world of schools, I am prevention.

Riddle 231

A strict stance on acts deemed wrong,

In my rules, no leeway long.

Not just a guideline, but a firm decree,

In my presence, boundaries be.

No drugs, violence, nor breach of peace,

In my realm, infractions cease.

A promise of safety, order, and respect,

In my law, conduct we inspect.

What am I, a rule so defined,

In the world of education, discipline entwined?

More than a policy, a deterrent clear,

In the landscape of schools, I'm severe.

Riddle 232

A shield against harm, a secure embrace,

In my care, a protected space.

Not just physical, but emotional too,

In my realm, well-being we pursue.

Preventing danger, ensuring peace,

In my plan, anxieties cease.

A foundation for learning, growth, and play,

In my guard, fears allay.

What am I, a priority so high,

In the halls of education, beneath my sky?

More than a concept, a commitment true,

In the journey of schooling, I'm due.

Riddle 233

Beyond the class, where passions ignite,

In my world, interests take flight.

Not just hobbies, but growth's fertile ground,

In my activities, talents are found.

Clubs, sports, arts, and more,

In my embrace, spirits soar.

A complement to academic life,

In my sphere, character is rife.

What am I, a pursuit so wide,

In the realm of education, where interests reside?

More than diversion, a developmental stage,

In the landscape of learning, I engage.

Riddle 234

Tools of the trade, for learners keen,

In my arsenal, knowledge glean.

Not just reading, but strategies profound,

In my application, success is found.

Note-taking, summarizing, questioning too,

In my practice, comprehension anew.

A foundation for academic achievement and might,

In my discipline, insights bright.

What am I, a set of techniques so fair,

In the world of students, essential ware?

More than habits, a learner's guide,

In the journey of education, I preside.

Riddle 235

The art of organizing, prioritizing the day,

In my system, efficiency's way.

Not just schedules, but a balance of life,

In my method, reducing strife.

Juggling tasks, deadlines, and rest,

In my practice, performing your best.

A skill for the student, and teacher alike,

In my discipline, productivity spike.

What am I, a strategy so prime,

In the realm of learning, against the climb?

More than planning, a life skill so grand,

In the landscape of success, I stand.

Riddle 236

A deep dive into texts, ideas, and art,

In my gaze, understanding's start.

Not just critique, but an exploration wide,

In my inquiry, no detail can hide.

Evaluating arguments, structure, and theme,

In my scrutiny, insights gleam.

A cornerstone of higher thought and debate,

In my practice, opinions articulate.

What am I, a method of thought so keen,

In the world of academia, often seen?

More than judgment, an intellectual dance,

In the realm of knowledge, I enhance.

Riddle 237

A look within, after lessons learned,

In my process, growth is earned.

Not just contemplation, but actionable insight,

In my practice, future's bright.

Connecting experiences, theory to life,

In my cycle, reducing strife.

A tool for personal and academic growth,

In my mirror, understanding's oath.

What am I, a learning style so deep,

In the journey of education, benefits we reap?

More than meditation, a transformative quest,

In the landscape of learning, I'm the test.

Riddle 238

Learning together, sharing the quest,

In my companionship, knowledge is best.

Not just study groups, but collaboration true,

In my interaction, insights accrue.

A mutual exchange, where teaching is shared,

In my circle, concerns are aired.

Enhancing understanding, confidence, and more,

In my community, abilities soar.

What am I, a method so grand,

In the realm of education, hand in hand?

More than companionship, a collective rise,

In the journey of learning, I'm wise.

Riddle 239

A repository of research, peer-reviewed and clear,

In my pages, new frontiers appear.

Not just articles, but knowledge's advance,

In my volumes, scholars' dance.

A dialogue of discovery, across the globe,

In my text, innovations probe.

A benchmark of scholarship, prestige, and more,

In my record, academia's core.

What am I, a publication so refined,

In the world of scholars, a treasure mined?

More than a magazine, a scholarly voice,

In the realm of research, I'm the choice.

Riddle 240

A culmination of study, a moment so key,

In my session, your work's decree.

Not just a presentation, but a rigorous test,

In my forum, your research is assessed.

Facing a panel, with questions and critique,

In my challenge, approval you seek.

A rite of passage, for the scholarly quest,

In my completion, achievements are confessed.

What am I, a milestone so vast,

In the journey of academia, at last?

More than a meeting, a scholarly feast,

In the realm of education, my beast.

Riddle 241

A gathering of minds, wisdom pooled,

Over a scholar's work, they ruled.

Guidance, critique, and support they lend,

On their approval, hopes ascend.

Not just advisors, but gatekeepers too,

In their hands, your academic debut.

A path to defense, they pave with care,

In their presence, scholarship we dare.

What am I, a panel so key,

In the realm of higher degrees, you see?

More than mentors, a critical assembly,

In the journey of research, I'm the embassy.

Riddle 242

A test of words, where knowledge is spoken,

In my arena, ideas are woken.

Not just a quiz, but a dialogue deep,

In my session, intellects leap.

Questions and answers, a dance of minds,

In my exchange, understanding binds.

A rite of passage in academia's quest,

In my challenge, your mastery's test.

What am I, an assessment so oral,

In the world of learning, a pivotal coral?

More than conversation, an academic rite,

In the landscape of degrees, I'm a knight.

Riddle 243

A broad test of all that's been learned,

In my scope, degrees are earned.

Not just a paper, but a marathon of mind,

In my trial, your limits find.

Covering subjects wide and vast,

In my survey, the net is cast.

A culmination of years in study's embrace,

In my completion, knowledge's trace.

What am I, a challenge so wide,

In the realm of education, a tide?

More than an exam, a scholarly feast,

In the journey of learning, I'm the beast.

Riddle 244

A grant of honor, supporting scholarly quests,

In my embrace, research manifests.

Not just funding, but a community of thought,

In my fellowship, innovation is sought.

An opportunity for growth, for work to delve,

In my tenure, your project you shelve.

A bridge to discovery, to explore and to learn,

In my award, accolades you earn.

What am I, a privilege so grand,

In the landscape of academia, a helping hand?

More than assistance, a scholarly pact,

In the realm of research, I act.

Riddle 245

A boon for inquiry, where questions meet aid,

In my support, discoveries are made.

Not just money, but a vote of confidence clear,

In my funding, your project's near.

From labs to libraries, fields to the net,

In my sponsorship, goals are set.

A catalyst for exploration, for data to find,

In my provision, progress is signed.

What am I, a resource so vital,

In the journey of knowledge, a cycle?

More than a gift, a foundation for quest,

In the realm of investigation, I invest.

Riddle 246

A group of learners, gathered by choice,

In my circle, multiple voices rejoice.

Not just study, but discussion and share,

In my gathering, insights bare.

A democratic space for learning to grow,

In my assembly, knowledge flows.

From books to life, subjects wide and deep,

In my fellowship, curiosity we keep.

What am I, a collective so wise,

In the landscape of learning, where dialogue flies?

More than a meeting, a communal quest,

In the realm of education, I'm a guest.

Riddle 247

A hub of collaboration, resources abound,

In my space, knowledge is found.

Not just a library, but a center more broad,

In my domain, learning's applaud.

Technology, study, and social interaction,

In my environment, satisfaction.

A flexible area, for minds to engage,

In my setting, the future's page.

What am I, an innovative space,

In the realm of academia, a communal place?

More than a room, a learning landscape,

In the journey of education, I take shape.

Riddle 248

A bridge to the community, knowledge to share,

In my program, care and prepare.

Not just teaching, but connecting and more,

In my effort, opportunities galore.

From schools to the public, learning extends,

In my mission, understanding blends.

A catalyst for engagement, for growth and for light,

In my pursuit, horizons bright.

What am I, a mission so broad,

In the world of learning, a welcoming nod?

More than instruction, a partnership's hand,

In the landscape of education, I stand.

Riddle 249

The bond between institutions and the world outside,

In my practice, doors open wide.

Not just outreach, but involvement true,

In my action, connections renew.

From service projects to partnerships in kind,

In my collaboration, mutual benefits we find.

A commitment to societal growth and well-being,

In my embrace, a shared vision seeing.

What am I, a synergy so grand,

In the realm of academia, a joining stand?

More than activity, a relational art,

In the journey of community, I take part.

Riddle 250

The flow of insights, from one to another,

In my process, discoveries uncover.

Not just teaching, but a sharing profound,

In my motion, boundaries unbound.

From research to practice, theory to field,

In my exchange, innovation's yield.

A bridge between generations, sectors, and more,

In my conduit, wisdom's store.

What am I, a movement so vital,

In the landscape of learning, a cycle?

More than dissemination, an intellectual dance,

In the realm of progress, I advance.

Answers

1. Teacher

2. School

3. Class

4. Student

5. Book

6. School Bag

7. School Bus

8. Blackboard

9. Homework

10. Textbook

11. Classroom

12. Principal

13. Lesson Plan

14. Curriculum

15. Exam

16. Quiz

17. Study

18. Lecture

19. Grade

20. Report Card

21. Education

22. Scholarship

23. Library

24. Notebook

25. Pencil

26. Desk

27. Assignment

28. Course

29. Diploma

30. Graduation

31. Tutor

32. Syllabus

33. Academic Year

34. Semester

35. Break (as in Spring Break)

36. College

37. University

38. Education Technology (EdTech)

39. Online Learning

40. Distance Education

41. Reading

42. Writing

43. Arithmetic

44. Science

45. History

46. Geography

47. Art

48. Music

49. Physical Education (PE)

50. Field Trip

51. Mathematics

52. Biology

53. Chemistry

54. Physics

55. Literature

56. Language Arts

57. Social Studies

58. Environmental Science

59. Computer Science

60. Information Technology (IT)

61. School Counselor

62. Extracurricular Activities

63. Debate Team

64. Sports Team

65. Club (e.g., Science Club)

66. School Play

67. Band

68. Choir

69. Assembly

70. Parent-Teacher Association (PTA)

71. Special Education

72. Inclusion

73. Learning Disability

74. Individualized Education Plan (IEP)

75. Gifted and Talented Education (GATE)

76. Standardized Test

77. SAT

78. ACT

79. Advanced Placement (AP)

80. International Baccalaureate (IB)

81. Tuition

82. Financial Aid

83. Scholarship

84. Fellowship

85. Internship

86. Thesis

87. Dissertation

88. Accreditation

89. Alumni

90. Undergraduate

91. Graduate

92. Postgraduate

93. Doctorate

94. Professor

95. Lecturer

96. Teaching Assistant

97. Research

98. Seminar

Don't miss out!

Visit the website below and you can sign up to receive emails whenever Said Al Azri publishes a new book. There's no charge and no obligation.

https://books2read.com/r/B-A-KSLCB-RXYWC

BOOKS 2 READ

Connecting independent readers to independent writers.

Also by Said Al Azri

Classics Reimagined: A Comedic Twist
Echoes of Venice: A Modern Tale of Redemption
Moby-Dick Reversed: A Whale's Humorous Account
Treasure Island: The Parrot's Perspective
Tom Sawyer: The Great Exaggerator
Blunderland Reimagined: Alice's Unique Perspective

Family and Parenting Dynamics
From My Heart to Yours: Messages of Love and Learning for My
Child
Balancing Family Life: Strategies for Modern Parenting

Heartstrings: Tales of Valentine's Verse
Verses of the Heart: A Poetic Journey Through Love's Whimsy
Verses of the Heart 2: A Poetic Journey Through Love's Whimsy

Life, Hobbies, and Careers Series
From Amateur to Applause: A Beginner's Guide to Stand-Up Comedy